USBORNE
PHILOSOPHY
FOR BEGINNERS

Written by
Jordan Akpojaro,
Rachel Firth and
Minna Lacey

Illustrated by
Nick Radford

Consultant philosopher: Dr. Alex Kaiserman
Designed by Freya Harrison

CONTENTS

What is philosophy? — 4
A world of philosophy — 6
Doing philosophy — 8
How to argue — 10
Thought experiments — 12
Why do philosophy? — 14

Chapter 1: Knowledge — 17
How do we know anything about the world around us – can we be sure that we know anything at all?

Chapter 2: The mind — 29
Is your mind somehow different from your body, and are you even in control of it?

Chapter 3: Beauty and art — 41
What is beauty, and what is art? And why is it so hard to answer these questions?

Chapter 4: God — 53
If there is a God, is it possible to prove that he or she exists?

Chapter 5: Politics — 65
Are there any rules that everyone can agree on that would make society a fair and happy place for everyone to live in?

Chapter 6: How to be good — 77
If you're not sure of the right thing to do, can the tools of philosophy help you to find an answer?

Chapter 7: Time and identity   93
Everything changes with time – but how much can
something change and still count as the same thing?
What is time, anyway?

Chapter 8: Logic and language   105
What are the rules of philosophy, and how can you follow
them if people don't always agree on what words themselves
actually mean?

Chapter 9: The meaning of life   113
Is philosophy merely a way of asking questions about the
world – or can it also be a way of life itself? Can it answer the
ultimate question: what is the meaning of life?

What next?	120
Multiple mysteries	122
Glossary	124
Famous philosophers	125
Index	126
Acknowledgements	128

USBORNE QUICKLINKS

For links to websites where you can find out more about philosophy,
famous philosophers including Socrates and Plato, and start thinking
like a philosopher with videos, games and activities,
go to **usborne.com/Quicklinks** and type in the title of this book.

Please follow the internet safety guidelines at the Usborne Quicklinks website.
Children should be supervised online.

WHAT IS PHILOSOPHY?

Philosophy is a way of thinking about things — from what the world around us is like, to what beauty is, to the existence of God. These are BIG subjects, and to get to the bottom of them, philosophers ask BIG questions.

But philosophy isn't just for philosophers. Chances are you've asked some of these questions yourself...

If I could take a pill that would make me happy all the time, should I?

How can I know that the Sun will rise tomorrow?

Should we treat all people equally, and if so, how do we do this?

Can I be sure that other people think, feel or see things as I do?

How do I know that this world isn't all a dream?

If there are aliens, do they have the same ideas about 'right' and 'wrong' as we do?

Can anyone prove that God exists?

Does outer space come to an end?

Is it possible to do absolutely nothing?

What makes something a work of art?

Is it right to help someone if I know that doing so will hurt someone else?

Why should we do what the government tells us? In fact, should we even have a government?

If scientists built a machine that behaved just like a human, would it have feelings, and should I treat it kindly?

Do animals have rights?

Some of these questions may seem like science fiction, but others can and do affect us in our day-to-day lives. This can mean anything from how we behave, to the way governments operate, to the laws we live by.

A WORLD OF PHILOSOPHY

Philosophy covers so many different questions that it's usually broken down into different branches. Here are just some of them, and a few examples of questions they deal with.

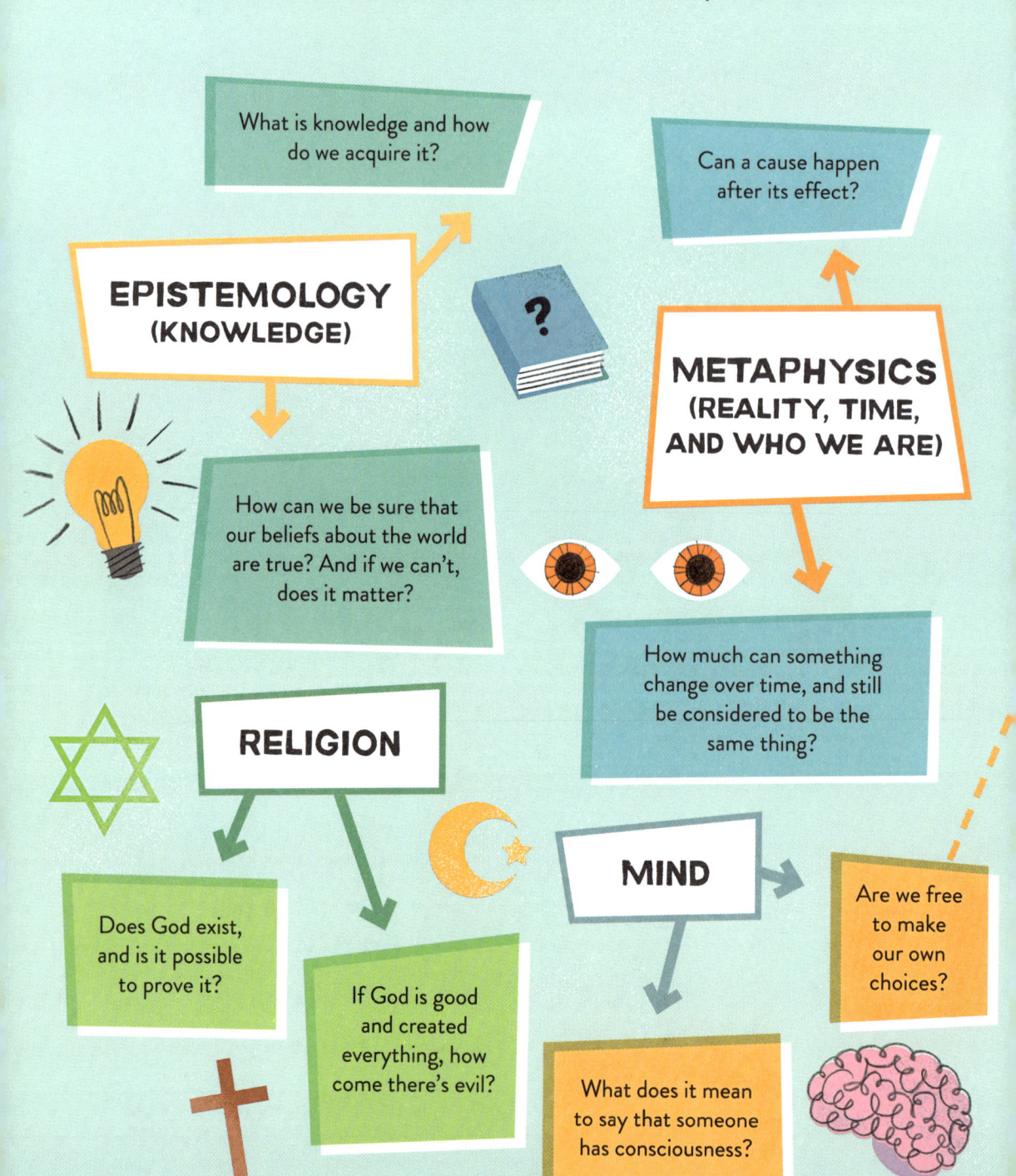

What is knowledge and how do we acquire it?

Can a cause happen after its effect?

EPISTEMOLOGY (KNOWLEDGE)

METAPHYSICS (REALITY, TIME, AND WHO WE ARE)

How can we be sure that our beliefs about the world are true? And if we can't, does it matter?

How much can something change over time, and still be considered to be the same thing?

RELIGION

MIND

Does God exist, and is it possible to prove it?

Are we free to make our own choices?

If God is good and created everything, how come there's evil?

What does it mean to say that someone has consciousness?

What is the morally right thing to do?

Why should we care about the environment?

ETHICS (ALSO CALLED MORAL THEORY)

Is *anything* right or wrong regardless of what we believe?

If I don't have free will, can I be responsible for what I do?

AESTHETICS (BEAUTY AND ART)

What is beauty?

What is art?

What is freedom?

POLITICAL THEORY

Can any sentences be both true and false?

What's the best sort of government?

Is it acceptable for people to own things?

LOGIC AND LANGUAGE

Is it possible to have a language that can only be understood by one person?

7

DOING PHILOSOPHY

Philosophers question EVERYTHING and ANYTHING. They question ideas and concepts, theories and arguments. They even question the questions that they and other philosophers ask...

So why ask so many questions? What's the point?

The point is that when you're doing philosophy, you can't take anything for granted.

What, not even things we're certain about?

No. *Especially* not those things.

Give me an example, please.

How do you know that the Sun will rise tomorrow?

Well, it always has.

OK. Now, can you imagine the Sun *not* rising?

Yes, I suppose so.

Since you can imagine it, surely you agree it's *possible* the Sun *won't* rise.

Um, yeeesss...

Well, if it's *possible*, you can't know for certain that it *will* rise...

Ok. But do I have to be certain? It still seems *likely* it *will* rise!

But does it being 'likely' give you a good reason to believe it?

> I don't get it!

> Don't worry. We can talk about the Sun rising again later (see page 107). The important point is, you seem to be getting the hang of doing philosophy.

> I do?

> Yes! The conversation we've just been having is philosophy in action. It's really not that difficult, especially when we use this question and answer approach.

The question and answer approach to philosophy has its origins thousands of years ago, in Ancient Greece. It's sometimes known as the **Socratic Method**, after the philosopher Socrates, who was famous for using it. In fact, the word 'philosophy' itself comes from an Ancient Greek word, meaning 'love of wisdom'. Here are two tips on how to do it well.

Socrates*

> Listen carefully when someone is putting forward an argument.

> Be polite. Even though it's called an 'argument', you can still present your ideas, or question someone else's, in a calm and cool-headed manner.

* say *sock-rat-ease*

HOW TO ARGUE

It's not enough to ask any old question when you're doing philosophy, you need to know how to argue properly. In particular, it's useful to know how to spot different ways an argument can be *true* or *false*.

Arguments are the key tools of philosophy. They're made up of two components: a **premise** and a **conclusion**.

PREMISE
A **premise** is a statement that can either be true or false.

CONCLUSION
A **conclusion** is a statement that's meant to follow from one or more premises.

If an argument is a good one, its premises give you good reasons to believe its conclusion. Here are some examples of arguments. Not all of them are good ones:

	PREMISE 1	PREMISE 2	CONCLUSION
A	All footballs are round.	This is a football. Therefore...	This football is round.
B	All people with brown hair have brown eyes.	This person has brown hair. Therefore...	This person has brown eyes.
C	All cats are animals.	My pet rat is an animal. Therefore...	My pet rat is a cat.

Philosophers examine arguments using a system of rules known as **logic**. If a premise is true, and the conclusion makes sense as a result of that premise, then it's a good argument. Now, you might have noticed that there is something wrong with arguments B and C. They're both *bad* arguments – for two different reasons.

B is a bad argument because one of the premises – premise 1 – is false.

> It's not *true* that all people with brown hair have brown eyes.

> Once you realize that premise 1 is false, you have no reason to believe the conclusion. When an argument fails in this way, it's said to be **unsound**.

C is a bad argument because the conclusion doesn't follow from the premises.

> I agree that premises 1 and 2 are true. But, even so, the conclusion doesn't follow from them.

> When an argument fails for this reason, it's said to be **invalid**.

> Logic is a very useful tool for examining philosophical and, indeed, everyday arguments. If you can explain *why* an argument is bad, it can help everyone to move forward.

THOUGHT EXPERIMENTS

Another one of philosophy's key tools is known as a **thought experiment**. This is a 'what if' question that sparks a series of further questions. Be warned, thought experiments can get you to imagine some very bizarre situations.

What if I wasn't walking around in a body, but was really just a brain in a jar that *thinks* it has a body?

What if you could save 10 people by killing one person. What would be the right thing to do? What if that person was your brother or sister?

What if someone went to prison voluntarily, and didn't *want* to leave their prison cell, would they still be free?

What if a tree falls in a forest and no one is around to hear it, does it make a sound?

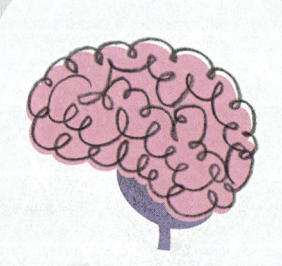

A good thought experiment should lead you onto a path of questions and answers that often challenge your first response to each experiment. The scenarios they describe don't have to be likely, or even physically possible, but they *do* have to make sense. It's no good asking someone to imagine a square circle, for example.

Here's a thought experiment that makes us question our ideas about identity.

> You say you've had this teddy bear for a long time. What makes you think it's the same as the one you were given as a baby?

> Well it looks the same... it has all the same parts.

> Ok, but what if, as time went by, the parts of the original bear wore out. And imagine that, over the years, each old part was replaced by a new part.

> Actually that's pretty much what did happen.

> Now, imagine this bear has *none* of the original parts. Can we really say it's the same teddy bear?

> I'm not sure, but I think so. Surely something can change but still be the same thing.

> Alright, but now imagine the original parts hadn't worn out, but were kept in a drawer. Then, years later, they were used to put together *a bear that looks exactly like the original one.*

> That would never happen!

> But what if it did? *Which* bear is the one you were given as a baby?
>
> The 'original' bear, made from replacement parts?
>
> Or the 'replacement' bear, made of original parts?

> Golly, I'll have to think about that...

Instead of a teddy bear, you could ask a similar series of questions about *yourself*. Find out more on pages 96-99.

WHY DO PHILOSOPHY?

Imagine you're part of a crowd watching someone give a speech. Chances are, a lot of people in that crowd are 'doing philosophy' without even realizing it...

> Scientists today say they have switched on the first artificial person. It's a robot with a brain that works just like a human brain.

> The robots are coming! And they're stealing our jobs. This is bad, very bad! Human jobs for human people!

> Why should I believe that news report? Sounds like science fiction to me!

> If their brains are the same as ours, aren't these robots essentially human?

> If someone switches that robot off, will they be killing it?

> What's so special about humans anyway?

> My smartphone is pretty clever. I wonder if it counts as a person?

> What's so bad about robots doing jobs?

> I, for one, welcome our new robot overlords.

All these people are responding to the news report and to the speech. Some of their questions might not have a clear answer, but just asking them, and debating them, could end up changing the future of society. This is an example of *practical* philosophy.

Does this mean that any time you ask a question, you're doing philosophy?

No. Not every question is philosophical, but lots are – especially questions that challenge very basic ideas.

Such as?

Such as, what do the words 'good' and 'bad' really mean?

And how can you know if something is 'good' rather than 'bad', or even whether it matters either way?

It all sounds a bit fiddly, and rather difficult.

Philosophy does have a reputation for being difficult. But most of the ideas in philosophy AREN'T difficult to understand – you just have to concentrate.

The exact words people use in arguments matter a lot, so philosophers listen and read carefully, and choose precise words, too.

Why bother?

Working through the arguments can take time, but it's fascinating, and very satisfying. And the process can help you understand real-world problems better.

Not everyone agrees that philosophy can fix problems. But people agree that it gives you thinking tools to sort out good arguments from bad in ANY situation.

15

- IS THERE A REAL WORLD OUTSIDE OF YOUR MIND? AND CAN YOU *PROVE* IT?
- WHAT'S THE MOST BASIC FACT YOU CAN THINK OF?
- HOW DO I KNOW IF THE THINGS I BELIEVE ARE TRUE?

KNOWLEDGE

When people talk about knowledge, they don't always mean the same thing. They might be talking about *knowing how* to do something, or *being acquainted* with someone or something, or *knowing that* something is true.

Philosophers are mainly interested in this last type of knowledge – knowledge of **facts**. Questions they ask include: how do we come to know things? What is knowledge anyway? Can we actually *really know anything*?

CAN WE REALLY KNOW ANYTHING?

The chances are you will want to answer, 'Yes, of course we can.' But there are some pretty powerful arguments that might persuade you otherwise. These are known as **sceptical** arguments. Their aim is to force you to doubt even what seems obvious and most certain. Here is an example.

Imagine there is a brain in a jar. The brain is hooked up to a supercomputer which feeds it all the experiences it would have if it were a walking, talking human being. In fact, the brain thinks that it *is* a walking, talking human being.

Brain in a jar

Cause of the brain in a jar's experiences (a supercomputer)

What the brain in a jar experiences

The brain in a jar's experiences are exactly like a regular person's. There's no way to tell them apart...

Reg (a regular person)

Cause of Reg's experiences (his senses)

What Reg experiences

...but the causes of the brain in a jar's and Reg's experiences are very different.

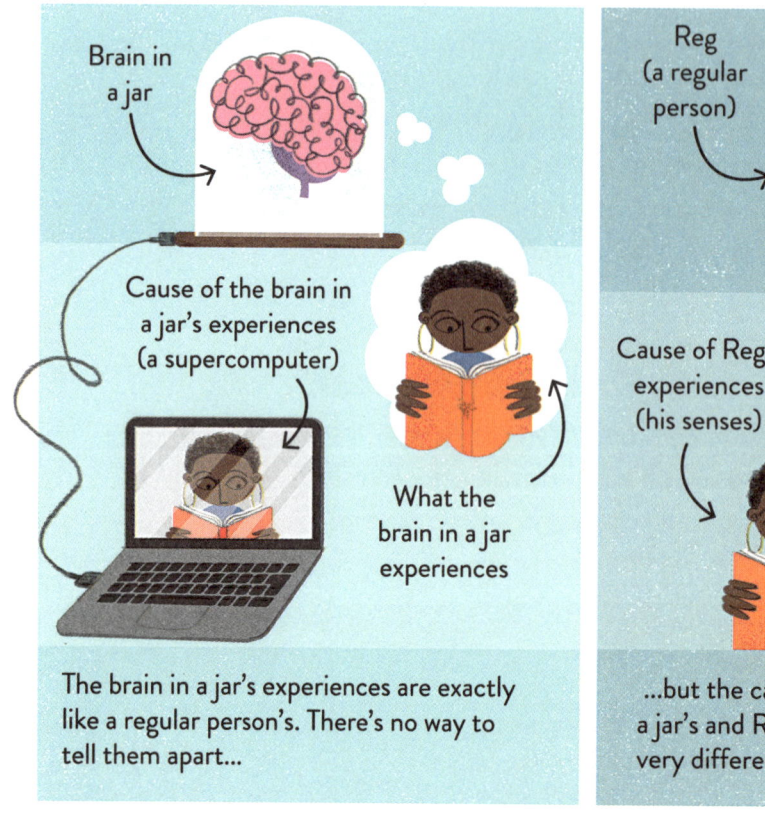

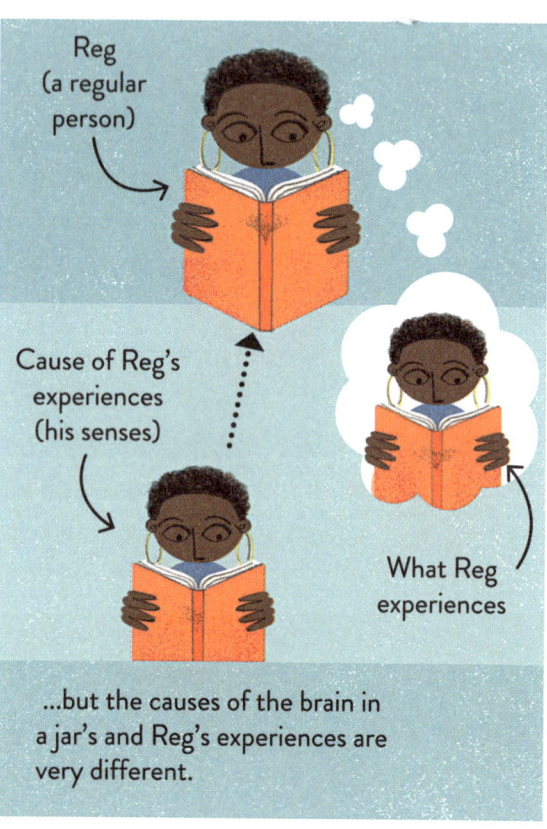

If the brain in a jar has no way of telling it *is* a brain in a jar, then how do you know that *you* are not a brain in a jar too? You don't.
The point is not actually to make you believe you *are* a brain in a jar, but rather to convince you that you can't be *sure* that you are *not*.

Well that's just ridiculous! It's *obvious* that I'm not a brain in a jar.

It may *seem* obvious, but how can you prove it?

For a start I've got fingers and toes and...

The computer could be just feeding you the *experience* of having fingers and toes.

It's no good appealing to your experiences at all, because they could *all* be caused by the computer.

What's the point of sceptical arguments? Well, if you can't *know* that you are *not* a brain in a jar, how can you be sure that reality is anything like what you think it is? And if you can't be sure of this, **how can you really know *anything*?** The answer seems to be that you cannot...

Common sense tells us that this argument just *has to be* wrong. But common sense sometimes gets it wrong, doesn't it? After all, people used to be convinced that the Earth was flat. Can we really rely on common sense to help us?

Here are some suggestions philosophers make *against* the sceptical argument.

The theory that our experiences come from ordinary physical objects – and not a supercomputer – is a simpler explanation. It makes sense to accept the simplest explanation.

Although it's *possible* I AM a brain in a jar, there is no good reason to think that I am. In fact, it seems pretty unlikely. True, I can't get rid of *ALL* doubt – but I don't need to do so to have KNOWLEDGE.

I don't need to prove that the external world exists. It's up to the *sceptic* to prove that it doesn't.

What do you think? Do you find any of these responses satisfying? Can you KNOW that you are not a brain in a jar, and if you CAN'T, does it really matter?

HOW DO WE KNOW THINGS?

Let's suppose that knowledge is possible. Although we can still make mistakes, it's likely that quite a lot of the things we *think* we know, we really *do* know. But how do we check whether having particular beliefs can count as knowledge?

- I know that J. K. Rowling has written a new book.
- How do you know that?
- Because I read it in the newspaper.
- But why does that make you think it's true?
- Well, because I think I can trust what I read in newspapers.
- But why do you believe *that*?
- Because, because, because... I just do!

The problem is, that this line of questioning needn't stop here. In fact, some philosophers argue that it could just go on forever, and ever and *ever*, in what's known as an **infinite regress**.

When you start to wonder why you believe something... there's always another 'why...?' and the endless chain of whys turns into an **infinite regress**...

- And why is this a problem?
- Well, if it's not possible to come to an end when trying to justify a belief, surely it's not possible to justify *anything* fully ever...

But there is an alternative...

Great! What's that?

Maybe not so great. Instead of going on forever, 'whys' and 'becauses' can turn back on themselves, making the explanation circular.

Ah, like this?

1 is justified by 2 is justified by 3 is justified by 1...

Is this *necessarily* a *bad* thing?

Well, it would mean that every belief you have can only be explained by another belief. If all beliefs are dependent on one another...

...no belief can be justified *absolutely*.

Ok so we can't really know anything. We are back to sceptical doubt!

Not necessarily...

Many philosophers think that we can stop this problem of regress *and* avoid circularity by thinking about the structure of knowledge as a whole.

Knowledge, they argue, is like a building. If everything we know is supported by a strong *foundation* of beliefs that can be trusted, the rest of our knowledge (if we are careful) will be sound.

I think, therefore I am.

My nephew is my sibling's son.

2 + 2 = 4

This grass looks green.

BUILDING KNOWLEDGE

The theory that knowledge is based on a strong foundation is known as **foundationalism**. Foundationalists don't always agree on exactly *which* beliefs form the foundations, but they *do* agree there must be beliefs that don't need to be justified any further. Such beliefs are known as **basic beliefs**. These can support other beliefs that philsophers describe as **non-basic beliefs**.

"Ok, so how does it work?"

"Start with the bottom brick. Each brick supports the one above it."

NON-BASIC BELIEF
I believe that my neighbour is now keeping sheep.

NON-BASIC BELIEF
I believe there are sheep in my neighbour's meadow.

BASIC BELIEF
I see white woolly animals in the meadow next to mine.

"There is, of course, room for error here. The sheep might have strayed into the neighbour's meadow, and actually belong to someone else."

However, some philosophers say that knowledge is not a building with foundations – it's more a web-like set of interconnected beliefs. As long as a set of beliefs is *consistent* (beliefs in the same set don't contradict one another) and it's *coherent* (all the beliefs support one another), then it's reasonable to have those beliefs. For instance, here's a set of beliefs belonging to a spider.

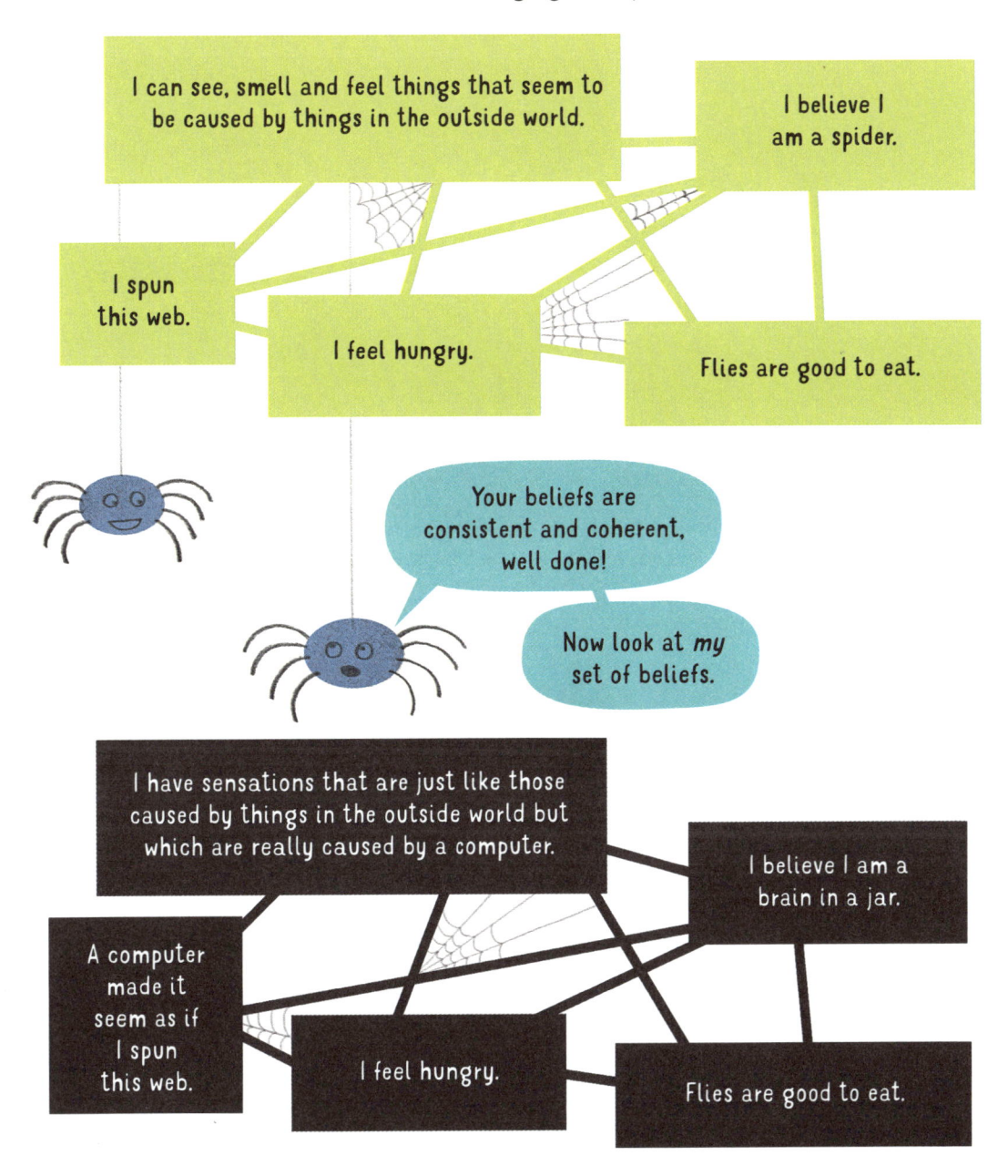

- I can see, smell and feel things that seem to be caused by things in the outside world.
- I believe I am a spider.
- I spun this web.
- I feel hungry.
- Flies are good to eat.

Your beliefs are consistent and coherent, well done!

Now look at my set of beliefs.

- I have sensations that are just like those caused by things in the outside world but which are really caused by a computer.
- I believe I am a brain in a jar.
- A computer made it seem as if I spun this web.
- I feel hungry.
- Flies are good to eat.

Both sets of beliefs are consistent and coherent. But they lead to two very different conclusions, and there's no way to tell which spider is correct. So, perhaps, even if all your beliefs are coherent, they could still be false beliefs.

WHAT IS KNOWLEDGE?

Most philosophers agree that in order to *know* a fact, that fact has to be *true*, and you need to *believe* that it's true.

> I believe that Peter can play basketball.

As long as this really *is* Peter, this looks like a clear-cut case of knowledge. But is this all there is to knowledge? Imagine this conversation:

> Did you hear that Khalid's latest song is the top-selling single this week?

> Yes, I know! I dreamt it last night.

> Er, really? OK. Well, *I* found out about it in this week's *Music Weekly* magazine, so that's how I know.

Jane

Bill

Suppose that Khalid's single really *is* the top-selling song. Does Bill really know this? Do you think Jane knows it?

If you think Bill doesn't know, but Jane does, then what's the difference between their two beliefs? Why does one count as *knowledge*, and the other not? The answer lies in the **reasons** they have given for their true beliefs.

Bill's reason for believing doesn't sound like a good one, while Jane's does. Philosophers would say that Jane's true belief is **justified,** but Bill's is not. So can we use this to give us a new and better account of what counts as knowledge?

> **To know a fact, that fact must be true, you must believe it and that belief must be justified (you must have good reasons for it).**

REASONS TO BELIEVE

Here's a new thought experiment: imagine Henry has dyed his hair blue.

Anna sees Henry in the street, and....

Henry   Anna

...forms a true belief that Henry has dyed his hair blue.

Meanwhile... Matt sees Eric, who happens to look *just like* Henry and has also dyed his hair.

Eric   Matt

He forms the true belief that Henry has dyed his hair blue.

Most people would say that Anna *knows* that Henry has dyed his hair. Seeing him in the street seems like a good enough reason to believe it. So her *knowing* fits the theory of knowledge as **justified true belief**.
 But what about Matt? Surely he *doesn't* know. Matt didn't see Henry, so his reason for believing that Henry has blue hair is only true by coincidence. So maybe we just need to add an extra condition to our definition of knowledge:

> **A justified belief must not depend on other false beliefs.**

Or, perhaps we just need to come up with a new approach to describing knowledge. Turn the page to find out more...

KNOWING HOW YOU KNOW

Some philosophers suggest that in order to know something, all you need is a **chain of causes** that links a *fact* to your *belief of that fact*. This is known as the **causal theory of knowledge**.

The causal theory can explain why Anna knows, but Matt doesn't. Anna knows that Henry has dyed his hair because her belief is *caused by* seeing Henry with blue hair. Matt's belief was *not* caused by this (it was caused by seeing Eric), and *this* is why he doesn't really know. The causal theory also lets you say that you know something, even when you can't justify your belief...

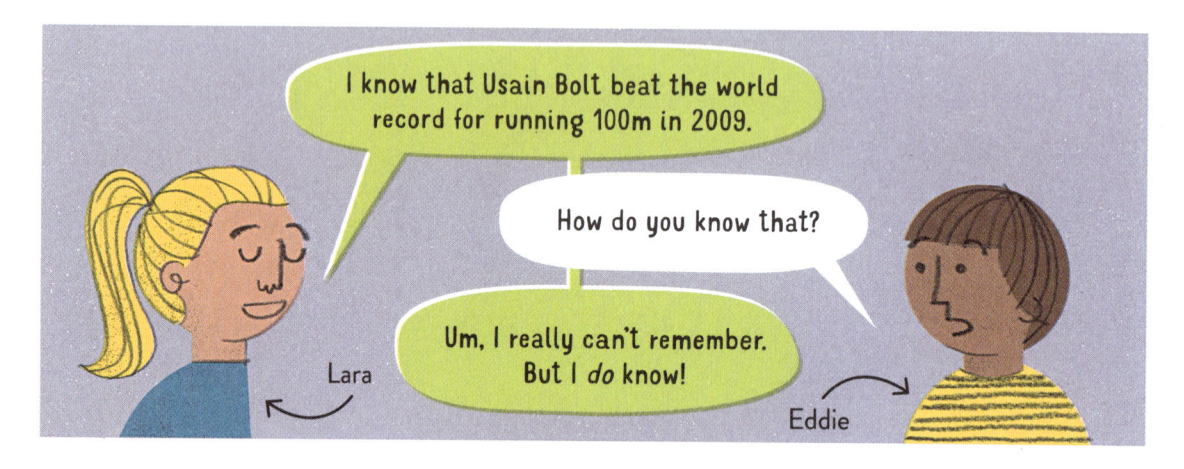

Lara: I know that Usain Bolt beat the world record for running 100m in 2009.

Eddie: How do you know that?

Lara: Um, I really can't remember. But I *do* know!

If you think knowlege is just justified true belief, you have to say that Lara *can't* know because she can't give good reasons for her belief.
But according to the causal theory, Lara *can* know as long as there is a chain of causes between the fact and the final belief. Here's an example.

| Event: Usain Bolt beat a world record in 2009. | The event is shown on TV news. | A journalist sees the news. | He writes a book about it. | Lara reads the book (but then forgets she has done this). |

So, so far, the causal theory looks pretty good. But, American philosopher Alvin Goldman came up with this thought experiment:

Amelia is driving through the countryside. She sees a barn and forms a true belief that there is a barn.

Amelia *seems to know* there's a barn because there is a causal chain between the barn and her forming a belief about its existence. Her belief is caused by seeing the barn, and seeing the barn is caused by the fact that the barn is there.

But, unknown to Amelia, there are lots of fake barns in the area, that look just like real barns. The barn Amelia sees *is* a real one, but she could easily have been looking at a fake one. If she had, her belief would have been false.

Fake barn
Real barn
Fake barn
Fake barn

So the question is, does Amelia really *know* there is a barn over there? It feels as if she only got it right by *luck*. If you think she doesn't really know, then the fact that there is a causal chain between her true belief and the barn being there isn't enough for her to 'know' it. So perhaps there's something wrong with the theory?

At this point you might think it's impossible to pin down what knowledge is!

For every theory philosophers have put forward, there seems to be another example that shows that the theory doesn't quite work.

This is something that often happens in philosophy. It may sometimes feel frustrating, but it's all part of the process.

Whether you think you've found a satisfying answer or not, let's hope you have clarified your thoughts and learned new things, too.

ARE YOU IN CONTROL OF YOUR MIND, OR IS IT IN CONTROL OF YOU?

ROBOTS DON'T HAVE BRAINS — BUT COULD THEY HAVE MINDS?

HOW DO I KNOW IF OTHER PEOPLE EXPERIENCE THE WORLD THE SAME WAY I DO?

THE MIND

Tackling questions about what our minds are, and how they relate to the world, is part of a branch of philosophy known as 'philosophy of mind'. Exploring different ideas about our minds can make us look at ourselves and other people in new ways.

DO OTHER PEOPLE HAVE MINDS?

It's often hard to know what's going on in other people's heads. We can describe what we *think* is going on, but we don't normally believe that we can actually see inside them. Sometimes this can lead to confusion.

I love hugging my dog. You know, it's the fuzzy pwar feeling!

What's she on about?

Philosophers sometimes describe people's minds as *private*. This means each person's thoughts and feelings are only accessible to *them*. So maybe other people's experiences are totally different from what you might expect.

Do we perceive the same things in the same way?

Do we mean the same things, for example, when we talk about feelings?

I feel great!

Me too!

In fact, how do you know if anyone else *has a mind at all*? People might *look* as if they have thoughts and feelings, but is it possible that they're just bodies with nothing going on in their heads?

You might say "Well, *I* have experiences, feelings and thoughts. Other people look and act like me, so, it makes sense that they have minds too." But this reasoning is actually faulty. To explain why, look at this example.

1. You see a brown dog.

2. You conclude that *all* dogs are brown.

All dogs *aren't* brown. The point is, it's not possible to make a *general* conclusion from only a *single* example. You need to show that the same thing applies in *multiple* cases. But you can't do that with minds, because you only know for sure that *you* have a mind.

Common sense lets us assume people *do* all have minds because it provides a simple and believable explanation for their actions. But why should we trust common sense? Well, imagine trying to explain people's behaviour at a party.

Explanation 1: everyone has minds that are similar to yours.

Of course those people are dancing. *Everyone* loves this song!

Explanation 2: other people don't have minds...

Err... if nothing is going on in their heads, why are they moving to that music? Creepy!

THE MIND-BODY PROBLEM

Many people would agree there are some clear differences between their minds and their bodies.

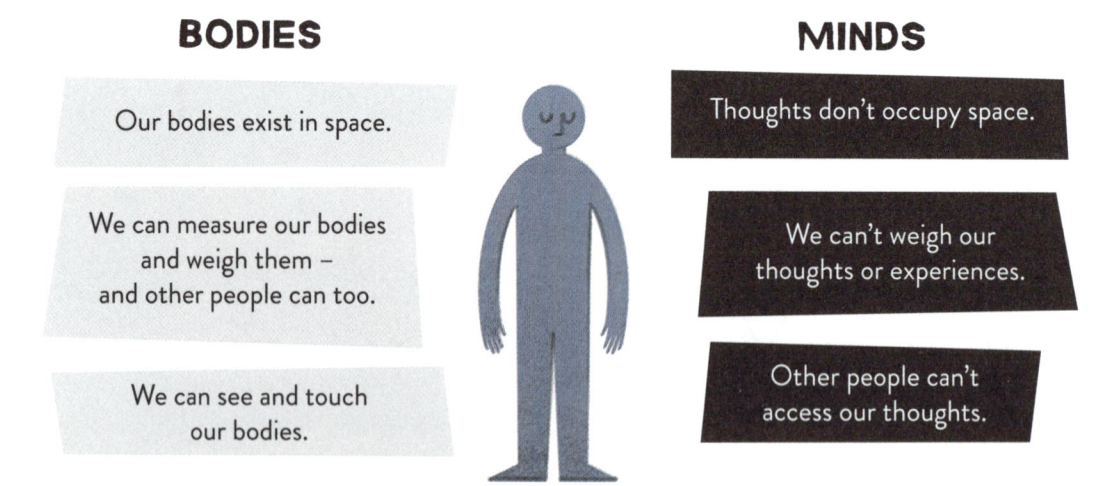

BODIES

Our bodies exist in space.

We can measure our bodies and weigh them – and other people can too.

We can see and touch our bodies.

MINDS

Thoughts don't occupy space.

We can't weigh our thoughts or experiences.

Other people can't access our thoughts.

So what is the relationship between your body and your mind? Philosophers call this the **Mind-Body problem**, and they've developed all sorts of theories about it.

1. THE MIND AND THE BODY ARE DIFFERENT SUBSTANCES

According to this theory, the body is a physical substance that takes up space, but the mind is not a physical substance, and it doesn't take up space. But then you might ask: how can a non-physical thing cause changes in a physical thing?

I want cake! — Non-physical thing (desire)

I will move my hand towards that slice of cake. — Physical thing (action)

Some philosophers say that something that doesn't take up space cannot affect something that does. So, for them, saying that the mind and the body are different substances doesn't solve the problem.

2. THE MIND *IS* THE BRAIN

Another way to describe the mind is to say that it's the *same thing* as the brain. Philosophers call this **identity theory**. The idea is that we can link what's going on in someone's mind (their **mental states**) to particular processes that are going on in their brain. Here are two rough examples.

What a brain scanner shows

When a person said they felt desire for cake (a mental state), *this* part of the brain was being used.

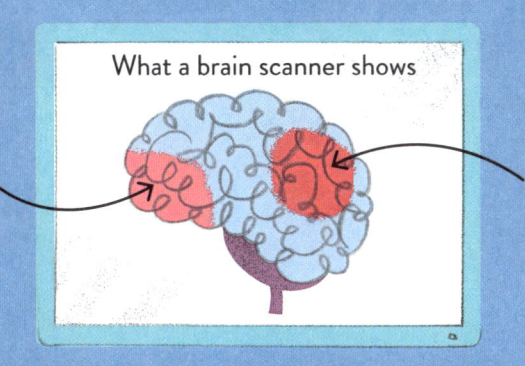

When a person said they felt pain (another mental state), *this* part of the brain was being used.

The idea is that every mental state is identical to a *specific* process in the brain. However, philosophers have pointed out a problem.

Many animals show signs that they feel mental states such as pain. But their brains can be very different to ours.

Since identity theory defines pain as a *specific* brain process, this logically implies that animals can't feel pain – or at least, the pain they feel isn't the same as the pain humans feel.

Here's a thought experiment. Imagine an alien with a completely different body. Do you think it could also feel pain?

Maybe it wouldn't even have a brain; maybe it'd have glowing goo in its head. But does that mean it can't feel the very same kind of pain we feel?

To solve the Mind-Body problem, philosophers need a definition of mental states, such as pain, that can work for *all things* that experience them. But if pain is linked to a specific part of the brain, it might suggest that things that *don't* use or have that part don't feel pain. Maybe identity theory is too specific.

33

3. THE MIND IS WHAT IT DOES

An alternative to identity theory is **functionalism**. According to this view, mental states should be defined in terms of what they *do*, or what their *function* is. We describe many everyday objects in this way.

For example, you might describe a clock as something that tells the time, regardless of what it's made from, or exactly how it works.

The time is 3 o'clock.

Mechanical clock · Digital clock · Sundial · Talking clock

But how can this be applied to mental states? Functionalists often compare minds to computers. Like a computer, the mind receives **inputs**, and responds with **outputs**. A mental state is just whatever causes an output in response to an input. In other words, what it *does* – its function – is to cause an output.

INPUT	MENTAL STATE	OUTPUT
DELICIOUS CHOCOLATE CAKE!	I WANT cake.	
Bolo sees an advert for cake. This sensation causes Bolo to...	...seek cake. This mental state causes...	...an action: Bolo tries to get cake (unless he wants something else more).

What makes a mental state what it is – here, wanting cake – is not some specific brain activity, but the fact that it *causes* a certain output – trying to get cake.

So, a functional description should work for *any* mind, whether it's a person, an animal, an alien or even a robot. Just as all clocks tell the time, different things can carry out the functions of minds using different materials. Here are some things that might carry out mental functions.

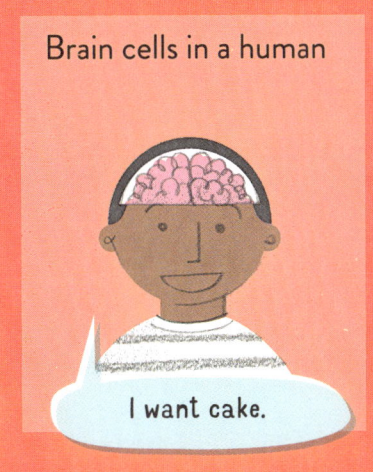

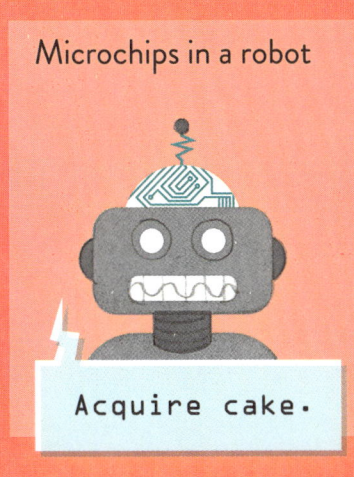

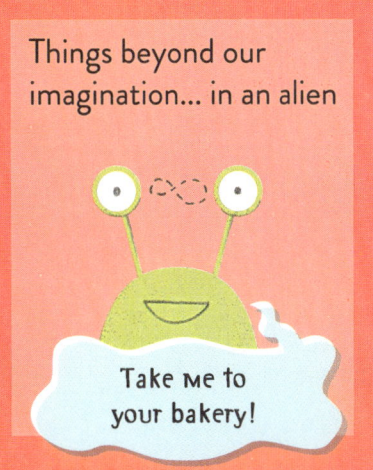

Brain cells in a human

I want cake.

Microchips in a robot

Acquire cake.

Things beyond our imagination... in an alien

Take me to your bakery!

But there are things functionalism *doesn't* explain. Desire and pain aren't *just* functions that bring about certain situations – they are things we *feel*. Ideally, functionalism could explain the connection between how mental states feel and their function – but it doesn't.

Some philosophers think it's impossible to explain the experience of mental states. Imagine trying to explain what pain is to an alien who can't feel it.

Have you ever stubbed your toe or bitten your tongue? It's really unpleasant.

It means you don't want to be in that situation again.

'Unpleasant'? What does that mean?

What? I don't get it.

I can describe it, but I don't think the alien will understand, unless it experiences what I feel.

If it's impossible to explain how things feel, then maybe it doesn't matter if functionalism doesn't explain feelings.

ARE YOU REALLY IN CONTROL?

Everyone makes choices every day. You *chose* to read this book (we hope). The idea of choice plays a big part in how we all think about our lives. Philosophers call this having *free will*. We often blame or praise people for their actions because they *chose* to do them.

You chose to graffiti that wall!

...erm I was... sleepwalking?

...so I wasn't in control of my actions?

DEFENDANT

Although we *think* we are free to act as we wish, is this really true? Some philosophers argue that we aren't free at all. If you think about the world around you, you might think that the present and the future are caused by past events. We explain all sorts of things by referring to past events.

How did your phone break?

An accident happened...

CRACK!

This idea is called **determinism**. If current and future events are determined by what's happened before, then that includes your actions and even who you are.

We can't change the past. But if the past *determines* the future...

...that means *we* can't control the future either.

In our own lives, there are many things that we tend to think we have no control over, because they were caused by events from long ago.

How you look depends on your parents, and how *they* look depends on *their* parents.

The language you speak depends on where you grew up.

Your ideas, beliefs and personality depend on what you've learned at school, from your parents, friends, or your surroundings.

Jak se máš?

Dobrý den!

Ahoj

Some people take this a step further. What if *everything* about you, and the world around you, depends on the past? If so, it must apply to your *choices* too. This is important. If none of your choices are made freely – if they're all determined by past events – it could affect how judges carry out justice.

The defendant is not guilty. A series of events forced his mind to make his body move in certain ways. He couldn't have chosen otherwise!

So here is the problem: If we couldn't ever have acted or chosen to act otherwise, how can we have free will?

37

IS EVERYTHING DETERMINED?

If everything we do is determined by the past, it looks as if we can't have free will. But what if the present and the future *aren't* determined by the past?

The science of how everything works is called physics. Some physicists argue that if you look really closely at the world, it turns out that *everything* that happens from one moment to the next is at least *in part* a matter of chance. Here's an example: flip a coin.

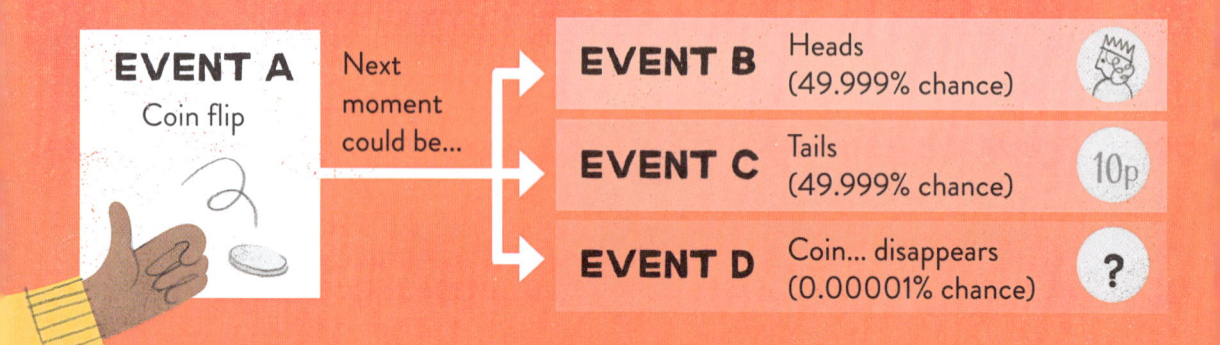

EVENT A — Coin flip

Next moment could be...

EVENT B — Heads (49.999% chance)
EVENT C — Tails (49.999% chance)
EVENT D — Coin... disappears (0.00001% chance)

What this means for *philosophers* is that it's always possible for something random to happen, even something very, very unlikely. If so, then determinism is false, because *some* events are not directly caused by previous events – they can happen at random.

So does that mean you have free will? Not necessarily. If determinism is false, your actions could be *completely* random. You might have no more control over them than you would if you made all your decisions with the help of a dice.

"What shall I do this afternoon?"

- Sleep
- Be lazy
- Make weird noises
- Eat
- Read philosophy book
- Mystery option

If your actions are random, this is essentially the same as having no control. So if your actions are determined, or completely random, you can't have free will.

38

However, it's very likely that in your experience you feel you *are* free to choose your actions. Is there a way to explain this? Well, what does 'free will' really mean? The simplest explanation is probably that you're free if you make a choice *without being constrained or limited* by the events of the past.

> That sounds reasonable, but I'm not worried about being 'constrained'. I think being free just means *getting to do what I want*.

> Well, if you think that, then there's no problem believing in both free will *and* determinism. It's possible that your actions were totally determined but you're still doing what you *want*.

> Hold on a second. Maybe I was wrong! For example, say I play video games all night, and I *feel* free and happy. If I don't have any other options to choose, then maybe I'm *not* free, even though I'm doing something I want.

> Now you're talking about *choosing from a list of actions*, instead of doing what you want and *feeling free*. Is freedom about how you feel inside, or what's going on outside?

> If freedom is about how you *feel*, then it sounds as if anyone can just decide to be free! As long as you feel like you're free, it doesn't matter whether or not your actions are determined.

> If freedom is about choosing actions, none of us are truly free — even if determinism is false. But it doesn't explain why I *feel* as if I'm in control of my choices...

> No matter what philosophers tell me, I still *act* as though I think I am free! That's good enough for me.

WHAT IS ART?

WHAT IS *GOOD* ART?

CAN A POEM OR A SONG BE AS BEAUTIFUL AS A ROSE?

BEAUTY AND ART

Questions about beauty and art fall into a branch of philosophy known as **aesthetics** (pronounced es-thet-iks). This comes from the Ancient Greek word *aisthesis* (es-thee-sis), which means knowledge through your senses: sight, hearing, touch, taste and smell.

WHAT IS BEAUTY?

Beauty can be applied to all sorts of things: people, music, poetry, art, mountain views, science, flowers, sunsets... but is it possible to pinpoint the meaning of a word that refers to so many different things?

Beauty could be...

...a sunny morning in spring.

...a piano concerto by Mozart.

...a red, red rose.

MULTIPLE MEANINGS

One idea suggested by philosophers is that the meaning of beauty varies according to the kind of thing it applies to. For instance, a song may have one kind of beauty that inspires a direct, immediate response.

But a poem could have a different kind of beauty that requires more time to understand and appreciate it.

This is a beautiful song. I loved it the moment I heard it.

I only saw the beauty of this poem after reading it three times and thinking about its meaning.

IS BEAUTY JUST IN THE MIND?

Some philosophers argue that beauty is purely in the mind of the beholder – making it what's called a *subjective* value. Others suggest that beauty is *objective* – it depends on qualities that exist *within* things. But if beauty is objective, what are the qualities that define it?

That woman is beautiful.

What do you mean by that?

Her beauty is *objective* – everyone can see it. She has big eyes, an elegant neck, shiny hair.

So you're defining beauty by the objective qualities she possesses. What about the sunset, is that beautiful?

Yes, of course.

But it doesn't have big eyes or shiny hair.

No it has different qualities. Dramatic, vibrant colours...

So are there any qualities that *all* beautiful things share?

No – that's impossible! At least, I can't think of any.

IF BEAUTY WERE OBJECTIVE...

In ancient times, philosophers identified qualities, such as proportion and symmetry, that appeared to define many beautiful things.
They believed if you could find a formula for the proportions of a beautiful human form, for instance, you could find a formula for beauty.

The beauty of this statue lies in the symmetrical features of his face.

And the harmonious proportions of his body.

If I copied these proportions, I could create another sculpture that was equally beautiful.

Architects in Ancient Greece used mathematics to construct beautiful buildings with specific proportions too.

They used a width-to-height ratio of roughly 1.62, known as the Golden Mean.

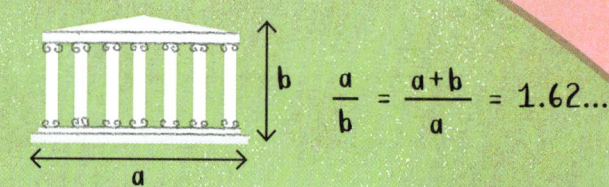

$$\frac{a}{b} = \frac{a+b}{a} = 1.62...$$

This building is beautiful because of its order, symmetry and proportions! Its width-to-height ratio follows the Golden Mean.

So any building with proportions following the Golden Mean will be just as beautiful.

But the Golden Mean doesn't explain the beauty of buildings with *other* shapes and proportions. So far, no one has found a rule that works for ALL beautiful buildings – let alone all beautiful things.

IF BEAUTY WERE SUBJECTIVE...

Now let's assume that beauty is subjective, and depends more on our own response to something. After all, there is huge variation in people's opinions about what is and isn't beautiful.

That dog is beautiful!

Really? I think it's very ugly.

That's fine. We all have different ideas about beauty and taste.

The problem with this argument is that if beauty depends purely on the viewer's perceptions, and it varies for each person, then two people can never know for sure whether they mean the same thing by 'beauty'.

That is a beautiful view!

Yes, it sure is!

But there still *is* a lot of agreement about what is and isn't beautiful. Few people would doubt the beauty of a dramatic sunset, for instance. This suggests that beauty *does* in fact have *some* kind of universal, recognizable meaning. We're back where we started.

WHO JUDGES BEAUTY?

German philosopher Immanuel Kant believed that beauty is subjective, but he also recognized that people use the term beauty in a meaningful way. Although it's impossible to find qualities common to *all* beautiful things, he argued that you *can* list the qualities *a person* needs to be a good judge.

> This is a beautiful work of art!

> How do you know? Why should I pay any attention to your opinion?

> I have studied art and visited lots of art galleries so I have the experience, and the good taste, to judge it...

Kant argued that experienced critics tend to agree with each other and can be trusted to make good judgements. They tell us what is good in literature, art, music and theatre, and select winners in competitions. Although there is variation in their taste, people tend to trust their opinion.

> Opinions are subjective, but the overall judges' score provides an *objective* value.

8.8   9.3   8.5

IS BEAUTY REAL?

Ancient Greek philosopher Plato linked 'beauty' to 'goodness' and placed both in an imagined ideal world outside our own. He thought beauty was an ultimate, objective value for people to strive for and that it didn't depend on anyone's views.

In fact, I think we can *never* see true beauty in this world.

What about this lily? I can see beauty in this.

It's a mere copy of the best possible lily.

Ooh, I want to see *that* lily!

Sadly I don't believe it exists for you to see. The most beautiful lily in the world is like a shadow made by an imaginary perfect lily.

But it seems odd to separate 'beauty' from 'beautiful things'. We *do* appear to experience beauty in our world and often share our experience of it with others.

PLEASURE AND THE SENSES

Ancient philosophers defined beauty by the pleasure or emotional response it inspired, which came from the senses.

This necklace is beautiful, because it gives me pleasure every time I look at it.

Yum! This ice cream gives me lots of pleasure.

Solving this maths puzzle gives me a slow, thinking kind of pleasure.

But the meaning of pleasure, like beauty, changes in different circumstances. Eating ice cream is a sensory pleasure, but it's not the kind of pleasure that comes from beauty. Other kinds of pleasure come from the mind, not the senses, such as reading or solving a puzzle.

WHAT IS ART?

In the past, art was often linked with beauty and the creation of beautiful things. Whether they find it beautiful or not, many people today have a general understanding of 'art' and refer to it happily in conversation.

Do you like art?

No, I love it!

Art here refers to drawing, painting... anything you might do during an art class at school. But 'art' can mean lots of different things...

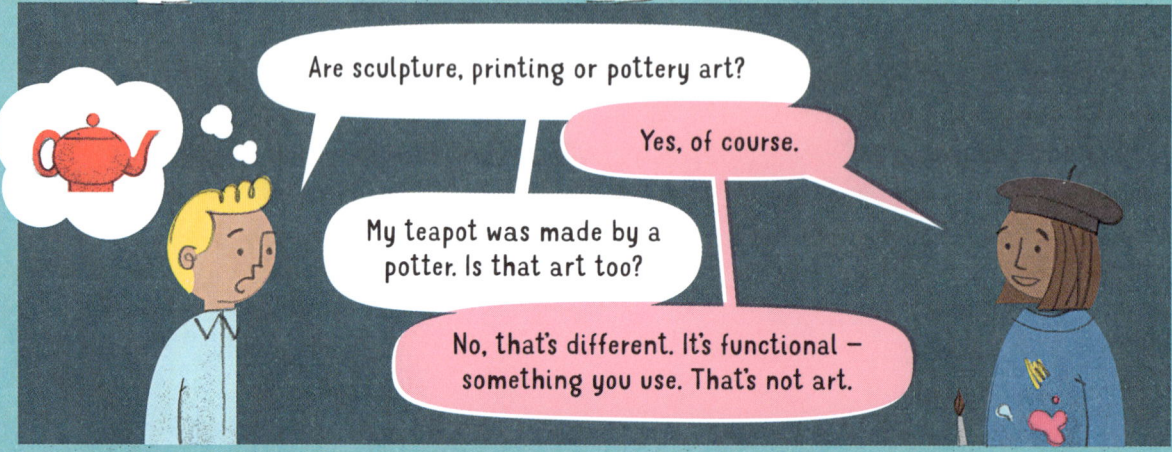

Are sculpture, printing or pottery art?

Yes, of course.

My teapot was made by a potter. Is that art too?

No, that's different. It's functional – something you use. That's not art.

Some people draw a distinction between objects that are *intended* to be art – such as a picture on a wall – and objects created for a function, such as a teapot or chair. But what happens if you put a functional household object in an art gallery? Can it *become* art?

Is my teapot art now?

Yes, I suppose it is.

Teapot
C. Grey, 2020

The 'art gallery test' is one way of defining art, but it doesn't cover everything. Lots of art is displayed outside galleries, on trees, hillsides or even in the swirls on the top of a cup of coffee. However you define art, it's always possible to think of an example that lies outside that definition.

ART AND MEANING

Over a hundred years ago, good art was often considered to be art that was beautiful, or art that showed subjects that looked very like things in the natural world. It was this that gave the art *meaning*.

It's a good picture because the tree looks so life-like!

But as artists began experimenting with abstract ideas, and painting pictures that didn't *look* like *things*, the meaning or subject became less clear. Some art, for instance, could be interpreted in lots of different ways.

I see a person reading the paper.

It's a bad dream.

No, it's a giant frog.

As non-representational art became more accepted, people began to ask whether art needed to have any meaning at all.

This arrangement of shapes is so... pleasing.

But it's not art. It's just a pattern. It doesn't mean anything.

Does that matter?

Despite these changes, art was still considered to be some kind of object created, or hand-made by an artist. But this idea was soon to be turned on its head…

49

PUSHING THE BOUNDARIES

In 1917, French-American artist Marcel Duchamp rocked the art world by submitting an upside-down urinal for an art show in New York. The urinal was titled 'Fountain' and signed 'R. Mutt, 1917'.

The gallery rejected 'Fountain' because it was not considered a true work of art. One reason was because it was not *made* by the artist. Others argued that it *was* art because Duchamp had given it artistic *meaning*.

Hands up if you think Duchamp's urinal is not a work of art.

Imagine if I put a sink in an art show. Would that be art?

Yes, if you chose it for a reason. You'd be like Duchamp, who took an ordinary object, named it and made us look at it in a new way.

Artists began to create work that wasn't necessarily intended to be pleasing, but to make people *think*.

This sparked a huge debate about what is and isn't art. This discussion returns every time new work is exhibited that pushes the boundaries of what art is considered to be. Consider a canvas painted blue or boxes printed to look like packets of soap you can buy in a shop. Do you think those would be art?

More recently, some artists have focused on themes of death, decay and horror, creating works of art that shock viewers. The publicity created is sometimes included in the work itself.

News Blood M. Lacey 2020

Imagine an artist displayed a bucket of animal blood in a gallery. Is that art? People now suggest art can be *anything* – anything an artist chooses to call art. It doesn't even have to be a 'thing'. Some artists put on a show, called **performance art**, that only lasts a few seconds.

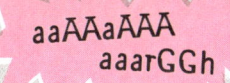

What just happened?

I don't know. It's performance art.

When trying to make sense of new art, it's easy to forget that many well-loved artists were highly criticized when they first showed their work. This suggests that whatever art *is*, its definition is sure to have changed by the time you've read this chapter.

IF GOD IS GOOD, HOW CAN THERE BE EVIL IN THE WORLD?

IS THERE ANY PROOF FOR GOD'S EXISTENCE?

DO WE NEED GOD TO EXPLAIN WHY THE WORLD EXISTS, OR WHY IT IS THE WAY IT IS?

GOD

Many religions are based around the idea that there is a God (or gods). Philosophical debates about God often focus on two basic, but very BIG questions: can we prove that God exists? And, conversely, can we prove that God does *not* exist?
The answer to either question will depend partly on what your idea, or concept, of God is.

Often, philosophers think of God as a single, superior being. Of course this *isn't* the *only* way to think of God, and you may not believe in God at all. But it's still worthwhile – and fun – to flex your philosophical muscles and examine the arguments.

THE IDEA OF GOD

God is often defined by theists (philosophers who believe in God) as a **perfect being**. But what does this mean? Does the idea of a perfect *being* even make sense?

'Perfect things' checklist

- ☑ Perfect square: 2-d figure with four equal straight sides and four right angles.
- ☐ Perfect book: er... um, not too long, not too scary?
- ☐ Perfect being: very, um, er, something...??!!

In fact, theists *have* typically put forward a number of qualities that they think a perfect being should have. For example, God should be...

OMNISCIENT
Knowing everything

OMNIPOTENT
Being able to do anything

WHOLLY GOOD

IMMORTAL
Will never cease to exist

EXTEMPORAL
Outside time and so not limited by time

UNCHANGEABLE

You might want to question whether these qualities really *do* make God perfect. But there are other questions to be answered too. What do these qualities involve? Are they compatible with each other? Do they even make *sense*? For example, let's take a closer look at *omnipotence*.

OMNIPOTENCE

Imagine there is a being called Bob. Bob is not God, but he *is* omnipotent. Bob can create things, change things, move things... You name it, Bob can do it!

Bob

TO DO LIST:
1. Flatten a mountain
2. Fly to Mars
3. Eradicate disease
4. Stop global warming

Bob *seems* to be able to do anything, *but* can he... create a stone that's too heavy for him to lift?

If Bob *can* make a stone he cannot lift, then there is something he *cannot* do – namely, lift that stone.

But if he *can't* make the stone, well, that's also something he cannot do.

Either way, it looks as if he can't *really* be omnipotent. This problem is called the **paradox of omnipotence.**

A **paradox** is a statement which seems false, even though it seems to follow logically from true premises (see pages 10-11).

WORKING AROUND A PARADOX

At this point, you could say, well, you can't expect even an omnipotent being to be able to do just *anything*. Take Bob's friend, Bodyless Bob. Bodyless Bob can do pretty much anything too, but since he doesn't have a body, he can't blow his nose, or drink a glass of water, or anything else that requires a body...

...but does that mean he can't be omnipotent?

Bodyless Bob
(You'll just have to imagine you can't see him.)

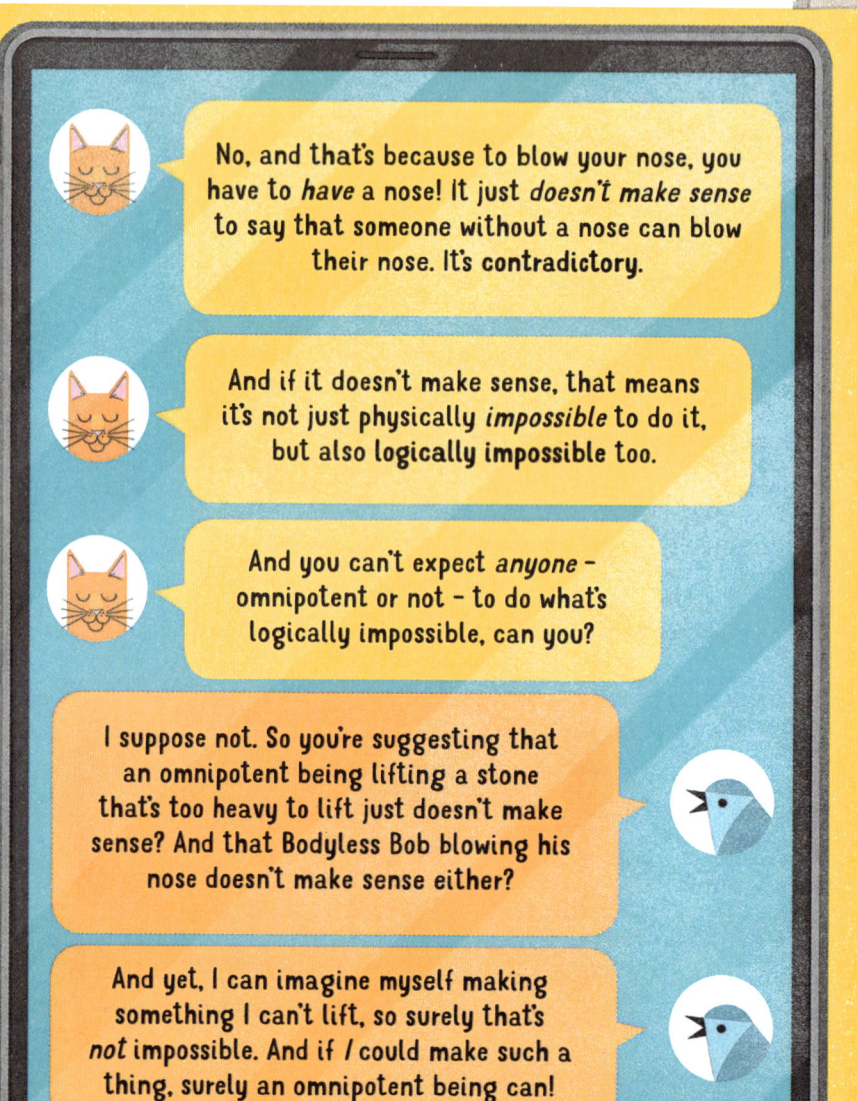

> No, and that's because to blow your nose, you have to *have* a nose! It just *doesn't make sense* to say that someone without a nose can blow their nose. It's **contradictory**.

> And if it doesn't make sense, that means it's not just physically *impossible* to do it, but also logically impossible too.

> And you can't expect *anyone* – omnipotent or not – to do what's logically impossible, can you?

> I suppose not. So you're suggesting that an omnipotent being lifting a stone that's too heavy to lift just doesn't make sense? And that Bodyless Bob blowing his nose doesn't make sense either?

> And yet, I can imagine myself making something I can't lift, so surely that's *not* impossible. And if *I* could make such a thing, surely an omnipotent being can!

56

"Look, *you* may be able to create something *you* can't lift, but that doesn't mean *Bob* can!"

"Fine, but if Bob *can't* make a stone he can't lift, then there is still something he can't do, so we are back to where we started!"

Meet Absolutely Impossible Bob

Absolutely Impossible Bob

TO DO LIST:
1. Everything on Bob's list
2. Make a square circle
3. Make 2 plus 2 equal 5
4. Create a stone that I can't lift (no problem!)

He can do absolutely *anything* – even the impossible.

"I'm not sure it fits in with my beliefs to say that God can do things that just don't make any sense."

Suppose you could agree on what it means for God to be omnipotent. It won't help you solve another problem – how do you combine omnipotence with God's other qualities? One of the most famous examples of this is known as the **problem of evil**. Turn the page to find out more…

THE PROBLEM OF EVIL

God is often said to be wholly good and kind. This seems to imply that God would never do bad things, or let bad things happen. But people do bad things all the time. If God exists and God is good, then how can he let them? This issue is known as the **problem of evil**.

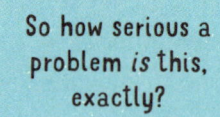

So how serious a problem is *this, exactly?*

Well, you could argue like this:
1. God and evil are logically incompatible – you can't have both.
2. We know evil exists, therefore...
3. God cannot exist.

The problem of evil is actually only a problem, though, if you also believe that God is omniscient (knows everything) and omnipotent, as well as wholly good.

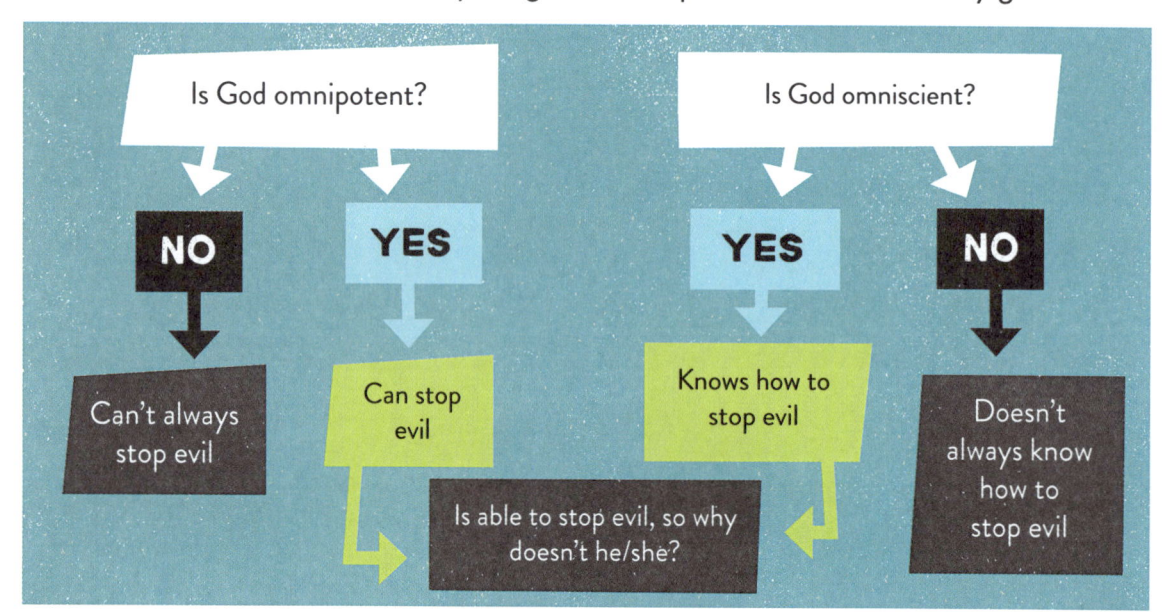

Is God omnipotent?

- **NO** → Can't always stop evil
- **YES** → Can stop evil → Is able to stop evil, so why doesn't he/she?

Is God omniscient?

- **YES** → Knows how to stop evil
- **NO** → Doesn't always know how to stop evil

What if being good and allowing bad things to happen *aren't* always incompatible?

My dad makes me go to bed early. That feels bad. But it's good*, because it means I won't be tired for school the next day.*

OK, so some *bad things can be good. But are they* all*? You'd have to explain how every single bad thing results in good, to solve the problem of evil this way.*

Some religious people DO say that bad things happen because God knows that a greater good will be the result. It doesn't matter if we just aren't clever enough to see it. But if you don't feel happy with this response, there's another version of the argument which altogether avoids the need to justify every instance of evil...

BEING FREE TO CHOOSE

In many religions, the idea of **free will** – people's ability to choose what they do with their lives – is very important. Some philosophers argue that free will is a great good in itself, and is so important that God wants people to have it. But as long as people have free will, it means they are able to choose to do bad things.

> So, as long as we have free will, it's possible that there will be evil. And that's why evil exists – it's not a mistake.

> Exactly!

> But not all bad things are caused by *people* doing evil. What about 'natural evils' – suffering caused by tsunamis, or fires? How could a good God let *them* happen?

> Hmm... Suffering can make us better people? Without bad things, there would be no need for kindness, compassion, forgiveness?

> Ok, but maybe we'd be better off in a world without those qualities if it meant there was no suffering?

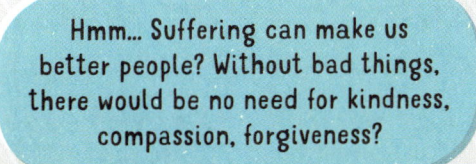

59

REASONS TO BELIEVE

Over the centuries, many philosophers have tried to show that there are good arguments, based on reasoning, for believing in God. Here's one that people sometimes give.

ARGUMENT FROM DESIGN

The world is beautiful and filled with creatures that seem to fit their environment extraordinarily well. It seems *incredible* that all of this could have come about by chance. Surely a better explanation is that someone intended things to be this way – and that could only be a being as powerful as God.

> Hang on. We don't need God to explain this! The theory of evolution explains how creatures came to be so well-suited to their habitats. It's part of nature.

> OK, but how do we explain nature itself, or why the Universe is the way it is? Surely it could easily have been different.

This line of thinking has given rise to the...

FINE-TUNING ARGUMENT

1. If the laws of nature had been even ever so slightly different, our reality would not have existed.

2. The probability of things being the way they are is very very very small. In other words, it's amazing that our reality exists at all.

3. It seems unbelievable that something with such a tiny probablility of existing could come into existence just by chance.

4. It seems more likely that something *intentionally* caused it to exist – and that is God.

> Now, here's a thought experiment to probe the fine-tuning argument:

Suppose that Tom wins the lottery. He had a one in 139,838,160 chance of winning the jackpot.

LOTTERY WINNER

Everyone thinks he is a very lucky man.

The next week, there are the same chances of winning the lottery and Tom wins it again.

Some people think he must be really lucky, but others are beginning to wonder if someone cheated.

And then the third week, the same thing happens yet again.

LOTTERY WINNER

> *No one* can be this lucky!

> *Someone* must have cheated!

When highly unlikely things happen, we often find it hard to believe that it's all down to chance, and tend to look for an alternative explanation, or reason.

> But, just because we *tend to* look for a reason, it doesn't mean there *is* one. I think your story tells us more about what people are interested in than it does about the origins of the Universe.

> And even if the fine-tuning argument could show that there is a designer, it *doesn't* prove that that designer is *God* as we think of him or her.

This isn't the end of the matter, of course. But if the argument from design for God's existence isn't convincing enough, there are several other arguments. Turn the page to find out about some of them.

ONTOLOGICAL ARGUMENT

Nearly a thousand years ago, a philosopher and monk called Anselm of Canterbury put forward what's known as the **ontological argument**. He said that there was something about the very *idea* of God that compels you to agree that God *must* exist. If you struggle to get your head round it, don't worry. The language is tricky:

Anselm's Proof

1. God is the greatest possible thing you can imagine.
2. Things can exist just in our imagination, or, in our imagination and in reality.
3. Things that exist in reality are greater than things which exist only in the imagination.
4. Suppose God exists only in the imagination.
5. This God cannot be the greatest possible thing.
6. So God must exist in reality as well as in people's imaginations. God must exist!

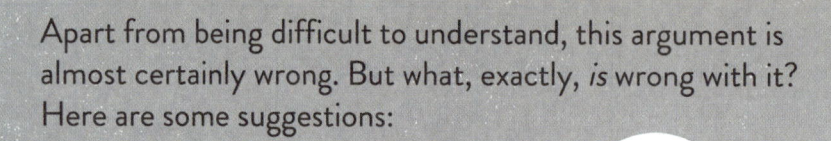

Apart from being difficult to understand, this argument is almost certainly wrong. But what, exactly, *is* wrong with it? Here are some suggestions:

- Do we have to define God as the greatest possible being?
- In what sense is *existing in reality* greater than *existing only in the imagination*? Does this even make sense?
- If you swap the word 'God' for, say, ice cream, couldn't you prove the greatest possible ice cream must exist?
- Isn't this argument just *defining* God into existence?

Here are some other arguments for the existence of God.

RELIGIOUS EXPERIENCE

Many people believe they have had religious experiences – experiences that *seem* to have been caused by God. These can be taken as evidence for the existence of God.

THE COSMOLOGICAL ARGUMENT

Everything must have a cause. But we can't have an infinite chain of causes. The causes have to stop somewhere, and with something that doesn't *need* a cause. The only possible candidate for that is God.

Another argument came from a 17th century French thinker called Blaise Pascal. He tried to convince people that believing in God was the most rational thing to do, even though it wasn't possible – in his opinion – to prove that God exists.

Pascal, like many people at the time, believed that if God existed and you didn't believe, you'd be punished after you died. If you did believe (and you were a good person), you'd be rewarded. Bearing this in mind, he invited people to look at all the possible outcomes of believing versus not believing.

Pascal's Wager	GOD EXISTS	GOD DOESN'T EXIST
BELIEVE IN GOD	When you die: eternal bliss	When you die: nothing
DON'T BELIEVE IN GOD	When you die: eternal suffering	When you die: nothing

Pascal felt that the possibility of eternal suffering was too great to risk. According to him, a rational person would bet on it being true that God exists, and do their best to believe it even if they didn't...

WHY SHOULD I LISTEN TO THE GOVERNMENT?

HOW CAN YOU TREAT ALL PEOPLE EQUALLY?

IS THE WHOLE IDEA OF 'PRIVATE PROPERTY' FAIR?

POLITICS

Politics is about how groups of people make decisions and work together. Whether it's a government running a country, people living together in a society, or some friends trying to organize an event – it all counts as politics.

Political philosophers are interested in what makes groups work in a peaceful and fair way. They explore different views about how society should be organized. It's not just about exploring ideas, though – political philosophers can and do influence how governments run their countries.

SHOULD WE OWN ANYTHING?

When people talk about things they own, whether it's a book or a bicycle or a house, they normally mean **private property**. This is stuff that a particular person or group uses. It's called 'private' because other people aren't allowed to use it without the owner's permission.

This farmland belongs to my family. You can't use it unless we say so!

Our family has a right to this land! We're willing to fight for it!

People often have disagreements about who owns what. Since private property causes so many disagreements, philosophers ask if it actually makes society better for everyone.

Here's one argument *for* private property. Imagine a group of fishermen are all fishing in the same spot.

If I use a big net, I can make a huge catch!

We don't want to lose out, so we'll start using big nets too.

At first, everyone catches loads of fish and business booms – but all too soon, there are no fish left. This isn't *just* a thought experiment. This has actually happened in seas around the world.

People in favour of private property claim that the fish ran out because the space wasn't privately owned – so no one took responsibility for it. If each fisherman (or group of fishermen) had their own private area, they'd have fished it responsibly, making sure there were always some fish left. Are these claims actually true?

1ST OBJECTION

The claim is that the space was ruined because it was shared. But actually, common property has been used responsibly throughout history. One of many examples is a Swiss mountain village that has shared a meadow for over 500 years – without ruining it.

2ND OBJECTION

You might also object that you think that private property doesn't make things better for *everyone*. Consider this counter-argument.

> Many countries waste a lot of food, while some people go hungry.

> If food was shared out, rather than being privately owned, people wouldn't have to go hungry.

> And since it's private, we can only share food if the people who own it are willing to share – and many aren't.

This argument doesn't prove that private property is always *bad* – just that we might not *need* it. And in fact some governments have tried to set up societies where some property – such as food and housing – is shared out. But deciding how to share things *fairly* is a whole new problem...

67

WHAT IS EQUALITY?

Most people agree that we *should* treat everyone equally. But it's not so clear what that means. While many people are unhappy with the inequality we see around us, it's not obvious what an equal society would look like.

STRICT EQUALITY

There are lots of different ways to look at equality. The most obvious idea is to treat everyone in *exactly* the same way and give everyone the *same* things.

EVERYONE GETS GLASSES

"I need glasses but my daughter doesn't. Isn't this wasteful?"

"Yeah! They've given us all the same glasses, but wearing them actually makes my vision worse!"

But everyone is different and has their own needs, so a one-size-fits-all approach doesn't make sense. *Equal* doesn't mean *identical* – we can treat people equally without necessarily treating them in exactly same way. Suppose we want to make sure everyone can enjoy a movie equally, we could...

"...give glasses to people with weaker eyesight..."

"...give hearing aids to people with hearing impairments."

"But there's no need to make changes for everybody."

This makes sense when all you're doing is watching a movie – we know we want everyone to be able to enjoy a movie. But what about a whole society? We know we want equality, but what *sort* of equality?

MEETING EVERYONE'S NEEDS

Here's one suggestion – meet everyone's needs equally. This doesn't mean giving everyone the same things, it means treating all people's needs as equally worth satisfying. According to this view, if someone doesn't already have access to something on the list below, it *should* be provided for them.

Shelter · **Healthcare** · **Water** · **Clothing** · **Food** · **Education** · **Toilets** · **Friends** · **Internet** · **A job** · **Family**

> If someone is struggling to get food, they should receive food. If someone is homeless, they should be given a home.

> And if someone already has what they need, then they don't receive anything.

> What about friends and family? These aren't needs; you *can* live without them.

> Really? I think friends and family are necessary, although I admit, I don't know how you'd make sure everyone had them.

> But aren't *needs* just what is *necessary* for survival? We can't just add any old thing.

Many people think that as long as no one has to struggle to survive, some kinds of inequality *are* acceptable – such as some people having more money than others. But others think just satisfying *basic* needs isn't enough. Other important things should be equal, too. Turn the page to explore other approaches to equality.

69

EQUALITY OF WELLBEING

Some philosophers think it's best to make everyone equally happy. This usually means meeting people's basic needs, then adding more things on top. Of course, each person's happiness will depend on different things, so different amounts of support would be given. But the aim is that everyone should be equally satisfied.

Sounds sensible? Well, consider this...

Expensive yachts make me happy.

Yeah, but we can't afford one... Do you really need a yacht to be happy?

Don't I deserve to be happy? Don't I deserve to have my desires fulfilled?

I think a yacht is an unreasonable demand.

THE YACHTFATHER

It's also difficult to put into practice. How do we tell if people are equally happy? We can't read minds...

I'm happy to pet her for another hour.

I mustn't let my boredom show.

Some people think happiness isn't entirely dependent on someone's situation.

I got the yacht, but now I have to sail it. Ugh. And Kelly has a bigger, more expensive yacht, so now I'm jealous.

Maybe it's just not *possible* to make people happy. Oh well, let's explore another possibility.

EQUALITY OF OPPORTUNITY

How about making sure everyone has the same opportunities? Some people don't have access to chances in life because of things that are beyond their control – such as where they were born. So the aim is to remove any barriers to opportunities so that everyone has a fair chance.

Here are some ways in which you could help everyone access education.

ACCESSIBILITY
Schools should be easy to access for students with disabilities.

GOOD LOCATION
Everyone should be able to get to school easily.

FREE SCHOOL MEALS
People shouldn't have to miss out on learning because of hunger.

SPECIAL NEEDS
Schools should provide trained teachers to help anyone with special needs.

NO FEES
People should be able to learn whether they're rich or poor.

Once these opportunities are in place, if things end up being unequal – some people get better grades, say – then that must simply be down to each person and... luck. Or is it? Consider this situation. Kay's parents are bilingual, so Kay learned to speak both English and Mandarin...

Kay has an advantage over lots of people, but it's not right for a government to stop parents from speaking to their children in their own language – is it?

That means I can access opportunities that aren't available to people who can only speak one language.

Working out how to share things fairly isn't easy. But there's one thing most people agree on. Even if we don't know exactly what equality looks like, it's unacceptable for some people to suffer and struggle to survive when we CAN do something about it.

LIMITING FREEDOM

In most societies, there are things no one is allowed to do. And many philosophers argue that it's OK to limit someone's freedom, if it's for their own good. This is called **paternalism**.

You have to wear a seatbelt in a car.

You're not allowed to go when the light is red.

Some of these laws seem so sensible that you probably don't object. But you might feel differently about laws which limit your choice in other ways. Most people want to *choose* how they live their lives – even if it's not good for them. Here's an example:

I'd like a super double cheese burger, with fries, nuggets and ice cream.

Well, you can't have them. They're bad for you. NEXT!

Some philosophers say it's simply not possible to do something good for someone against their will. But there seem to be cases when paternalism might well help people.

My laptop is in there!

You can't go in. It's too dangerous!

Creating hard rules, such as traffic light laws, is known as **hard paternalism**. According to another idea, known as **soft paternalism,** it's only OK to limit someone's freedom if that person is *unaware* of what they are doing.

> Do you realize that the meal you've ordered is bad for your health?

> Yes. But I still want it.

> Ok, you know what you're getting into.

> One unhealthy meal coming right up!

Soft paternalism lets adults have their freedom and protects them when they don't know what they are doing. One reason you might object to this, is if you think something else might be more important than an individual's freedom.

> Finally, I can eat my unhealthy meal.

> NOT SO FAST!

> They might be softies, but I'm not. You need to think of other people! If you get sick, it gives doctors like me extra work, and that costs money.

> I think it's OK to limit your individual freedom if it's for everyone's benefit. Your health affects everything – from your family to your doctors – so I'm confiscating this food.

Most people are OK with *some* paternalism. But others worry that if rules limit people's freedom to choose too much, society can become too controlling and even dangerous. All societies limit people's freedom a little, since everyone has to follow *some* rules. But who sets the rules?

WHO SHOULD SET THE RULES?

Most countries are run by governments – people with the job of creating new laws, or getting rid of old ones. They're also allowed to use force to make people do what they say. But why is it OK for the government to do this, and not other groups? Consider this scenario.

We've got a law-breaker on our hands!

You broke our laws!

We're going to lock you up in our basement!

Don't you know wearing purple and green looks bad? You have to dress properly!

Wait, you aren't the police. You don't even work for the government. Who are you?

We're the fashion police! We've drawn up our own laws and we're going to enforce them – for your own good!

WHAT?!

Very few people would accept a random group of people making laws and forcing everyone to follow them. But the government does this, so what's the difference? The difference is a matter of **legitimacy** – the government is *allowed* to make laws and enforce them. But why? What makes them so special?
Why *should* you obey the law and listen to the government?

NO, WE *SHOULDN'T* OBEY THE LAW

Some people, often known as **anarchists**, believe that we have no duty to obey the government. They think there's no real difference between a government-run police force and random law-makers.

> The government isn't legitimate because it tells people what to do and uses force to make them do it. We don't need a leader. Our society should simply work together.

> But how can we organize ourselves without a leader?

> Most groups of friends don't have leaders; that's anarchy at work! Why don't we try it on a larger scale?

> It might work with friends, but what about people who *don't* get along?

YES, WE *SHOULD* OBEY THE LAW

Some philosophers think that a government is legitimate because citizens have *agreed* that it is. They argue that citizens voluntarily agree to obey laws, and allow the police to enforce them, for their own protection. This is often known as **the social contract**.

> Hang on! I was born into this society, but I don't remember agreeing to any contract.

> If you accept the way society is, and let the police keep you safe, then I count that as agreement.

> But then I can't refuse! If I *disagree*, I'll end up in jail. I don't really have a choice...

> Well, you *would* agree if you had to live in the wilderness or in a lawless society.

> It doesn't matter if I *would* agree. What matters is whether I agree now!

> Ok then, why *don't* you agree?

While it's hard to define what counts as an agreement, this idea explains why most of us accept the rule of law. Put simply, if you think it's better to live with other people, rather than going it alone, it makes sense to agree to follow some rules.

IS IT EVER OK TO LIE?

IS FIGHTING EVER JUSTIFIED?

ARE THERE SOME MORAL RULES THAT EVERYONE SHOULD OBEY?

HOW TO BE GOOD

How should we live our lives? How should we act with friends, family, strangers, people who give us orders or people who serve us?

In all areas of life, there are accepted ways of behaving, known as **moral codes**, that define how we are supposed to act and treat the people around us. The branch of philosophy that examines these codes and helps us make decisions about the right thing to do is called **ethics**. Ethics looks at values, such as rights and duties, that help make the world a better, fairer place.

MORALS – ARE THEY ANY USE?

Moral codes are like rules that tell us what to do and how to behave. They give us tools for making decisions, taking responsibility for our actions and dealing with all sorts of tricky issues.

"Hi, Fred, can you come round on Saturday afternoon?"

"Ooh yes, I'd love to! Oh, no, wait a minute – I promised to visit Grandma with my mum."

Fred has made a promise – a commitment to do something, which is a kind of moral rule. He now has to decide whether he's going to keep the promise or not.

Some people think that there is a moral rule against breaking promises, or even asking to do so. But others suggest it depends on the situation.

"Mum, Stan's asked me over on Saturday, can I go?"

"Oh ok, we can visit Grandma on Sunday instead."

I'm happy that Stan has asked him round.

In this example, Fred has asked to break his promise, but his mother is happy to change their plans. Having a rule helps you make decisions, but it doesn't always give you a clear answer about what to do.

WHY SHOULD I?

'Ought' or 'should' are words that often appear in rules or moral statements. Some of these 'oughts' and 'shoulds' are practical, not moral.

> You ought to do up your shoe laces.

> Why should I?

> Because if you don't, you might trip and hurt yourself.

But other 'ought' statements *are* moral. They are also trickier to justify.

> You ought not to kick people.

> Why not?

> Because it's wrong to hurt people.

> I know people say that, but *why* is it wrong?

> Well, if you go around hurting people, they might do the same to you. Imagine if everyone did that...

> So the reason for not hurting people is to protect myself?

> Not just that – how other people *feel* matters, too. The world is a *better place for everyone* if people don't go around hurting each other.

> So *if* I care about others and want to live in a world that's a better place for everyone, *then* I ought not to hurt other people.

> Yes.

Here, the final reason given for not kicking people depends on a belief, or assumption, about the world. Wanting to live in a world where people don't harm one another is a good reason for following a moral code.

WHERE DO MORALS COME FROM?

My aunt says it's wrong to be cruel to animals.

So, is it wrong just because she says it is?

No! It really is wrong.

So it's wrong in itself, and she just recognizes that it's wrong?

I suppose so...

Most people pick up moral codes throughout their lives – from family, school, religion, books and the media. But is it reasonable to judge things merely on the grounds that someone *says* that's how it is? Can you trust that person as a source of moral knowledge? Or is it better to work out what's right and wrong for *yourself*?

Some philosophers argue that religion is like a giant thought experiment. People assume that morals come from God or some kind of higher being, who automatically has more authority than someone's aunt.

According to my religion, God says it's wrong to envy our neighbour's house.

Is it wrong simply because God says it's wrong? Or does God say it's wrong because it is *wrong – independently of God?*

I think it's wrong in itself. We should be grateful for our little hut.

I think it's wrong because God says its wrong.

Some people do think moral rules are true simply because God says so. Others think morals are weaker if they are true *only* because God says so. It's as if morals are valued more highly if they already exist somewhere out there, so we can learn to recognize them. But is it possible that morals exist independently of humans, or God? Surely someone has to create them?

WHY BE GOOD?

Most people tend to try to do the right thing, at least *some* of the time. Acting selflessly – caring for others more than ourselves – is considered morally good. But is it possible to act truly selflessly, or do we always do things that will help ourselves in some way? Some philosophers argue that many acts that appear selfless can hide a selfish motive.

> I'm going to tidy my room.
>
> *If I tidy my room, Dad will be happy and might buy me an ice cream.*

> Can I help you?
>
> *If I'm kind to others, they might be kind to me back.*

> Do you want to join us?
>
> *If I'm friendly to Sandra, she might invite me to her party.*

If you believe that any act of generosity will be returned, can it be morally good? Helping others can make you feel good inside, but does that mean it's *not* morally good? If the reward is no more than a sense of goodness, then most people would agree that a selfless act is morally good – and that there *are* plenty of *selfless* acts.

> That stranger is lost, I'll show her the way.

> I'll help that old man cross the road.

> I'll give this money to charity.

To help decide if an action is right or wrong, philosophers have developed ways of looking at morality. Some have very formal names, such as **utilitarianism**, **deontology** and **virtue ethics**. Read on to find out more about them.

THE PURSUIT OF HAPPINESS

When faced with a moral dilemma, how *do* you decide on the right course of action? One solution is to choose what causes the greatest benefit, or the greatest happiness, for the greatest number of people. This idea is known as **utilitarianism**.

Utilitarianism focuses on the *consequences* of an action, in particular, the *number* of people that will benefit from it, and *how much* they will benefit.

MORE HAPPINESS

If the total amount of happiness gained outweighs some sadness by a smaller group of people, then a utilitarian would say it's morally right to do this thing.

WHAT ARE ITS ADVANTAGES?

It provides a clear way to judge whether an action is morally right or wrong.

It doesn't treat different groups of people differently – it's purely about numbers.

It makes people more morally responsible, to consider the *consequences* of their actions.

Most people agree that increasing happiness and reducing harm overall is a worthwhile outcome.

Utilitarianism is often used to make big government decisions - for instance moving a small number of people from their homes to build an electric dam that benefits thousands.

What utilitarianism doesn't do is consider the rights or implications for the few, the people who might not benefit from an action.

WHAT ARE ITS DISADVANTAGES?

It justifies the suffering of a few, to achieve the happiness of the many.

Happiness means different things to different people.

How do you define happiness, let alone compare one person's happiness to another's?

How much happiness will result is not always easy to predict.

Surely all individuals have rights. Utilitarianism doesn't consider anyone's rights.

LESS HAPPINESS

Sometimes, what you feel is the right thing to do is not always what the majority wants, or what gives the most happiness.

A majority of millions could kill a minority of thousands and feel justified, just because it makes the majority happy.

83

JUDGING ACTIONS

Another way to make a moral decision is to focus on the action, not the consequences. This is known as **deontology**. It's about following rules and doing the right thing. Imagine you had to decide whether to betray your best friend to save the class from being punished.

I've got two options. To betray Finn or not, that is the question.

I think it's wrong to betray a friend, so I'm choosing this option.

Betray friend → He will be punished

Don't betray friend → Whole class will be punished

Deontologists who believe strongly in loyalty might choose *not* to betray a friend, even if it leads to 30 people being punished. One problem with this philosophy is how rigid it can be. It doesn't allow for your opinion about what is right or wrong to change, depending on the circumstances.

If you don't tell me who did it, then the whole class will be expelled and they'll all fail their exams.

Hmm, maybe I should betray my friend after all?

Focusing on actions, the choice is between betraying a friend or not. But if the class received an extreme punishment, or if your friend had done something worse than you'd imagined, being loyal might not *feel* like the right choice any more. Maybe sometimes we have to judge morals on *intuition*, or *what feels right*.

DO WHAT GOOD PEOPLE DO

Another way to make a moral choice is to imagine how a good or virtuous person would act. This is known as **virtue ethics**. For this to work, it's necessary to define what it means to be good. Here's a list of things a good person might be expected to be or do:

- Kind and helpful
- Respects others
- Always places others' needs first
- Fair
- Works hard
- Always honest

Not sure I know anyone with ALL these qualities...

Even if you could agree on what qualities a good person should *have*, here's another problem. Virtue ethics doesn't provide a reliable method for finding out what would be the right thing to *do*.

Shall we knock down four people's homes and build a big park? Or keep the houses and build a small park?

Alan the gardener was wise and good. What would Alan have done?

I have no idea! What would Alan have done?

If Alan is not there, it's not clear exactly how to come to a decision.

RULES ARE RELATIVE

Different families have different ways of doing things. So do different schools, regions and countries. Some philosophers suggest that moral judgements are only true or false in relation to the community you belong to. So a moral rule can be true for one place, and false for another.

I have two husbands.

It's acceptable in our community.

In our country, it's wrong for women to have more than one husband.

Is having two husbands wrong? If you are a moral relativist, you think there is no single answer to this question. Having two husbands can be wrong from one perspective, and right from another.

But couldn't two people from different communities disagree about what the right thing to do is? It's a bit like disagreeing with someone about which way is left. You both understand what 'left' means. You might both be pointing left. But if you're facing each other, you'll be pointing in different directions.'

This way is left!

No, this way is left!

One problem with moral relativism is that there are some actions that seem wrong *regardless* of what anyone else thinks. For instance, even if stealing or torture are accepted in some places, most people would want to say that they're wrong, not just *for us*, but wrong *full stop*.

The opposite of relativism is the idea that moral beliefs are either true or false. This is known as **absolutism**. For an absolutist, it makes no difference which community you belong to. If cannibalism is wrong, for example, then it's wrong whichever community or time in history you are from.

We eat human meat in our village, would you like to try some?

No! That's wrong!

ARE SOME RULES FOR EVERYONE?

The belief that there are at least some universal moral rules that should be upheld across all communities has led to many international agreements, including **The Universal Declaration of Human Rights** (UDHR).

Children should not be made to work as slaves. Does everyone agree?

Yes!

Created in 1948, the UDHR sets out a list of rights for *everyone*. It aims to make the world a fairer place, where humans can live with dignity and respect. Agreements like this are often backed up by international laws. However, these laws only apply to the countries that sign up to them.

TEST YOUR ETHICS

Here's a thought experiment. A runaway train is hurtling along towards ten people who are tied to the track. **You** control a switch that can send the train onto a different track. But if you do, one person will die.
WHAT SHOULD YOU DO?

Ten people's happiness outweighs one person's happiness. I'll pull the lever and kill one person to save ten.

The choice is between killing an individual or doing nothing. It's wrong to kill, therefore it's wrong to pull the lever. It's not my fault if 10 people die.

You can make the choice harder by imagining that the single person is a relative or friend. Or, instead of pulling a switch, what if you had to push a person onto the track to stop the train? Could you do it? **Perhaps there is no right answer here?**

PHILOSOPHY ON THE ROAD

Self-driving cars need programs to instruct them how to react in different situations. Designers of self-driving cars are working with philosophers to write those programs.

Should a self-driving car swerve and kill one person to save three people in the road?

And should the car swerve off a cliff, killing the single *passenger*, to avoid hitting three people in the road?

BEWARE CLIFF!

Most people answer 'Yes' to the first question and 'No' to the second, even though the consequences are the same. Should a self-driving car act in a utilitarian way that saves more people, or in a way that protects the passenger first? Or should self-driving cars simply be banned? Philosophers are hard at work looking for solutions to these problems.

DIFFICULT DECISIONS

Life is full of moral questions that people – including philosophers – disagree on. Here are some examples.

THE RIGHT TO DIE

Some people believe that if you are very ill you should have the right to die sooner with the assistance of a doctor. Others say this is suicide, which many people believe is wrong. Does your belief depend on the action, the consequences, or on something else?

- I am dying of cancer and in great pain. I want the doctors to help me die.
- What if the pain and sadness is temporary? The doctors may find a new treatment...
- A doctor could abuse the system to commit murder.
- Assisted suicide is against my religion.
- Life is a fundamental 'right' and no one should have the power to take it away.
- The kindest solution is to relieve the patient of their pain and suffering.

CAPITAL PUNISHMENT

Should the state have the right to take a person's life if they have been convicted of murder?

- What if a prisoner really is innocent? Innocent people have been wrongfully accused of crimes.
- If someone commits a serious crime, they lose their rights, including their right to life.
- The threat of execution is the best way to scare people into not committing serious crimes in the future.
- The state has a duty to help convicted criminals become better people, no matter how serious their crime.
- No one, not even the state, has the right to take someone's life.

MEDICAL ETHICS

Doctors have to face all sorts of ethical dilemmas on a daily basis.
There are groups or committees in hospitals that help make these decisions.

This child needs emergency treatment, but his parents are not here to give permission for the operation. Should we wait?

My patient told me she had committed a crime. Should I inform the police?

PRIVACY

My emails, phone and internet use should be private. I have the right to privacy.

I don't mind what the state does if it helps prevent a terrorist attack.

WAR

Is it ever ok for one country to declare war on another?

War is justified if it's the only way to stop a country from attacking and killing my fellow citizens.

Violence always leads to more violence. Countries should always look for a peaceful solution.

Killing is wrong. War is never justified.

We should go to war if it's the only way to stop an evil dictator from killing thousands of people.

Innocent people always die in wars.

MAKING LAWS

It's hard to find answers that everyone agrees on. Every country has to consider the arguments for and against these types of things, in order to make decisions and laws about them. Laws can differ widely from country to country. At times, your personal viewpoint may be different from the laws of the country you live in. Some people who disagree with laws campaign to get them changed.

> HOW DO I KNOW THAT YOU ARE THE SAME PERSON I MET YESTERDAY?

> WHAT IS TIME?

> DOES IT MAKE SENSE TO THINK I COULD GO BACK IN TIME AND CHANGE THE PAST?

TIME AND IDENTITY

Time and identity are two thorny subjects that are discussed in a branch of philosophy known as **metaphysics**. Metaphysics deals with all sorts of problems – some of them very BIG ones – including the idea of existence, reality, space, the properties of things, and cause and effect. In this chapter, you will just get a small taste of this wide-ranging area of philosophy.

IDENTITY

What makes one thing the same as another? How do you explain how something can change and still be the same thing? These are questions about **identity**.

'The same' can mean two things, and it's important not to confuse them. The first type of identity is known as **qualitative identity**. Imagine two cars that have just rolled off the production line.

They both have the same

Type of engine

Latest tech

Shade of yellow

CAR 1   **CAR 2**

These cars have all the same qualities. They are exactly alike, or *qualitatively* identical. But they are *still* two separate cars.

Now, imagine you buy Car 1, but then it's stolen. One day, the police tell you they've found your car. It doesn't *look* like your car, but they assure you that it *is*. The thief has...

...sprayed it red

...switched the hub caps.

This car looks slightly different so it's *not* **qualitatively identical** to the original car. But it *is* **numerically identical** to it. This means there is only one car and it is the very same as the car you bought. What enables us to say that the car at one point in time is the same car as at another time – especially when it has changed?

Well, the car hasn't changed much. It would be silly to say that just *painting* it means it's gone out of existence and been replaced by another car.

Ok, but what if it had changed more radically?

Perhaps you might think that as long as something changes *gradually*, it can continue to exist, even if it changes a lot. Remember the thought experiment about the teddy bear on page 13? Here it is again, using the car.

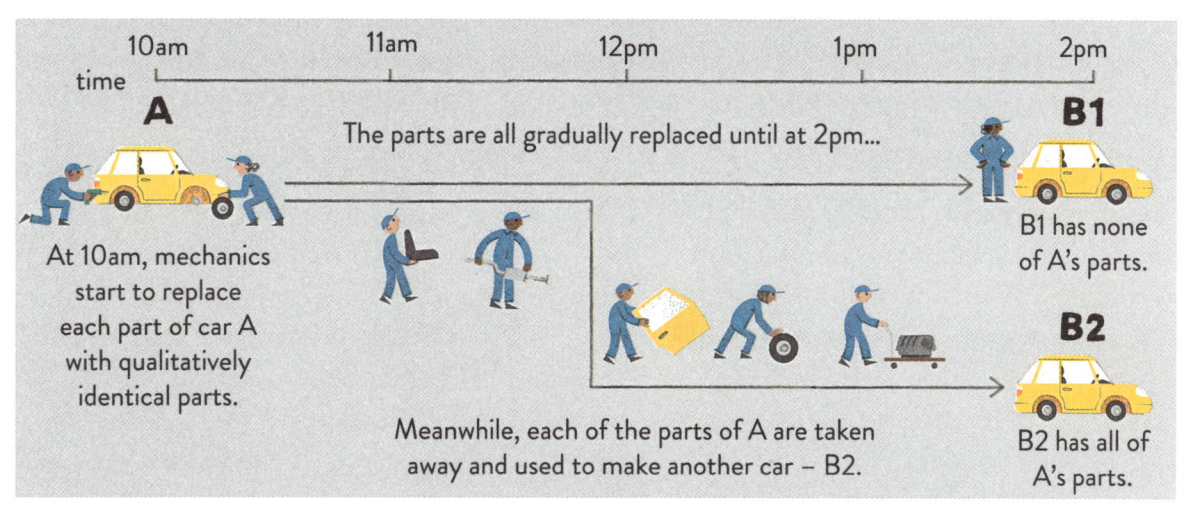

time: 10am, 11am, 12pm, 1pm, 2pm

A — At 10am, mechanics start to replace each part of car A with qualitatively identical parts.

The parts are all gradually replaced until at 2pm...

B1 has none of A's parts.

Meanwhile, each of the parts of A are taken away and used to make another car — B2.

B2 has all of A's parts.

By 2pm, there are two cars, B1 and B2. These two cars are qualitatively identical to each other. They are also both *exactly like* the original car, A. But which one is *numerically* identical to A? They can't *both* be, can they?

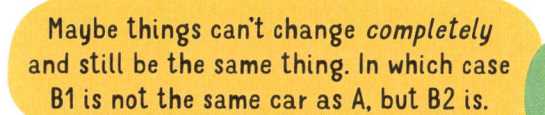

> Maybe things can't change *completely* and still be the same thing. In which case B1 is not the same car as A, but B2 is.

> Fine, but at what point between 10am and 2pm does car A cease to exist, and B1 come into existence?

> Hmm, ok well maybe it's B2 that's not the same as A, then. It's a different car that just happens to be made of the original parts of A.

> But what if all the parts from A were taken away, and used to make B2, but *not* replaced? Then B1 would not exist. Would you still want to say B2 is *not* A?

> Alright, well maybe they *are* both A then!

> But B1 and B2 are two distinct objects. They can't be numerically identical.

If this all seems tricky, things get even trickier when you start to think about identity in relation to *people*. Turn over the page to find out how and why.

95

PERSONAL IDENTITY

When it comes to people, the problem of identity gets a bit more complicated. For a start, what counts as a person? A human being? A brain? A mind? Or something else...? Here's a simple-sounding question that philosophers ask: How do I know that I am the same person as the person who started reading this book? Answering it, though, is far from simple.

SAME BODY?

We tend to assume that if someone's *body* continues to exist, then *that person* continues to exist too. This is how we *tell* that someone is the same person from one moment to the next. But does this mean that what *makes* you the same person, from one time to another, is that you have the same body? Is **personal identity** the same as **bodily identity**?

Here's a thought experiment to help you test out this idea.

Sam has a serious accident. Her brain is fine, but the rest of her body is dying.	New techniques make it possible to remove her brain without damaging it...	...and transfer it into a new body, where it works as well as it used to. But is this still Sam?

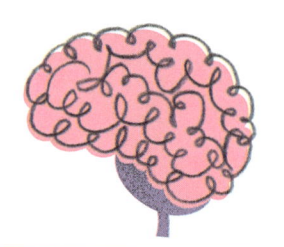

If you think it *is* still Sam, the chances are it's because you don't think that she – or what makes Sam *Sam* – is the same as her body. Or, not her *whole* body, at least. Some philosophers have suggested that what makes someone the same person from one time to another is *having the same brain*.

SAME BRAIN?

If Sam is identical to her brain, then the person who wakes up after the operation is still Sam because they have the same brain. Sam goes wherever her brain goes. But here's a fact to chew on. Our brains are made up of two parts, or hemispheres, that can operate independently.

So, what if it were possible to...

...take one hemisphere out of Sam's head...

...and put it in a new head (without damaging it.)

Which of the resulting people, if either, would be Sam?

Hmm I'm not sure about this. Surely what makes me *me*, is not some slab of physical stuff, but rather my thoughts, feelings and other mental states.

Yes, and we also tend to think of these mental states as happening in the brain, so as a matter of fact, my mental states – and thus I – go where my brain goes.

But what if you don't need this very brain in order to be you? What if you could have your mental states in a different brain, or a computer, even? Would you *be* that computer or brain? If you think the answer is yes, then this probably means you think that what makes a person the same person at different times is not brain identity, but something to do with the *mind*. But what does this involve? Turn the page to find out.

SAME MIND?

Some philosophers have argued that **continuity of consciousness** is what makes someone the same person from one time to another. But what on earth does this mean? One argument says it's all to do with your memories.

How does this work?

Imagine that Ruth – in 2031 – claims that she's the same person as someone who was called Jo in 2011. On the continuity of consciousness view, Ruth can only be the same person as Jo if she can remember experiences had by Jo in 2011.

> But surely that's not going to work. What if Ruth *can't* remember everything – or even *anything* – Jo experienced? Does that mean Ruth *can't* be Jo?

> After all I can't remember much of what *I* experienced when I was five. And, at 80, I may not be able to remember anything at all. But I'm still the same person, aren't I?

> That's ok. You don't need to remember *everything*, as long as there are overlapping sets of memories.

AGE 5   **AGE 21**   **AGE 50**

But there's a problem with using memories to define identity – it's circular.

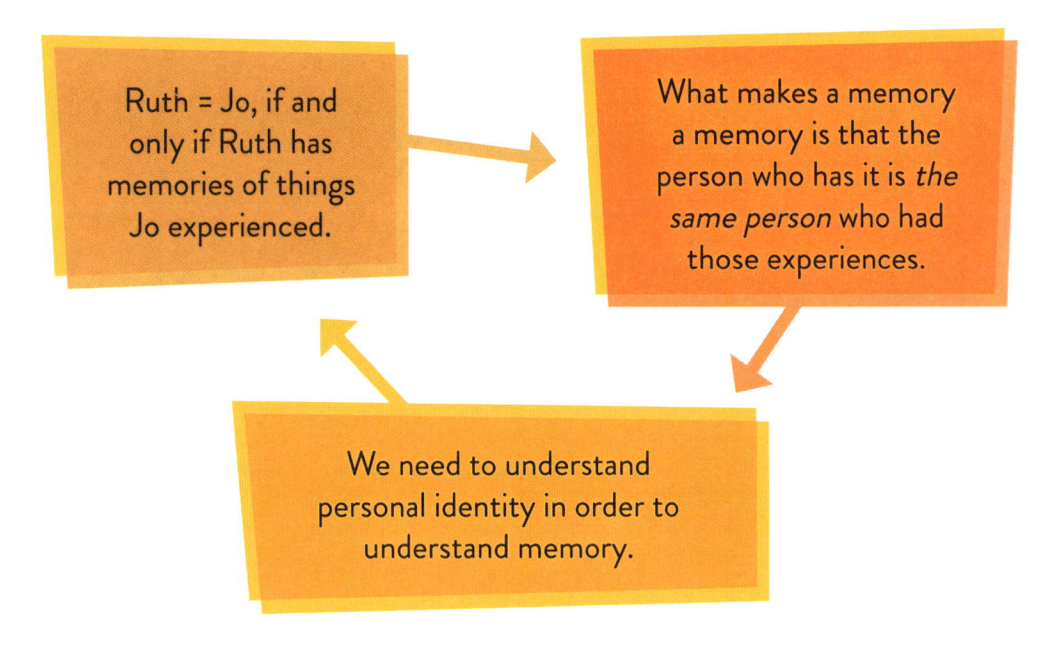

> Ruth = Jo, if and only if Ruth has memories of things Jo experienced.

> What makes a memory a memory is that the person who has it is *the same person* who had those experiences.

> We need to understand personal identity in order to understand memory.

The idea of memory assumes you already have an idea of what personal identity involves. You'd be using personal identity to *explain* personal identity.

Here's another thought experiment. At the moment it's science fiction, but one day it might become possible.

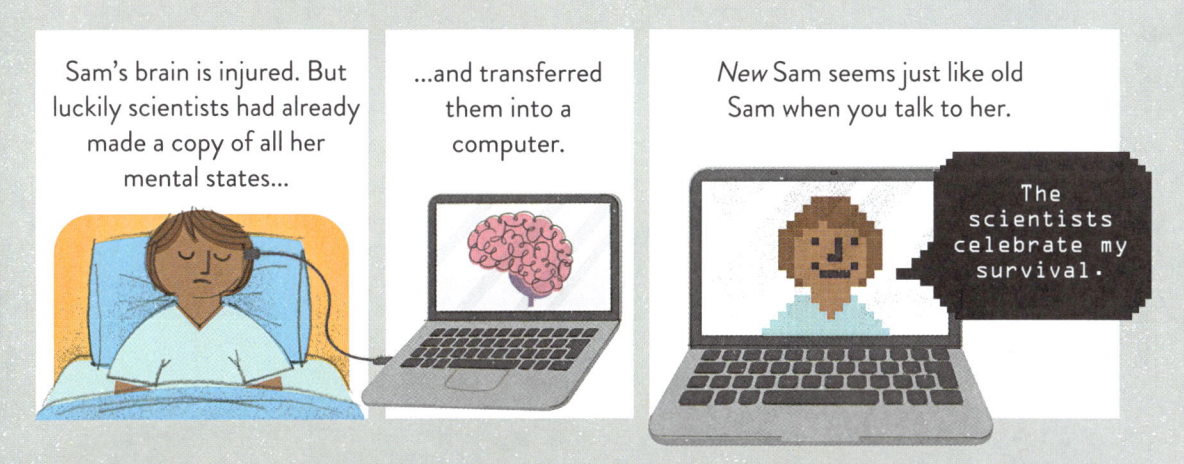

| Sam's brain is injured. But luckily scientists had already made a copy of all her mental states... | ...and transferred them into a computer. | *New* Sam seems just like old Sam when you talk to her. |

> The scientists celebrate my survival.

Of course, the procedure is only a success if you think that copying Sam's mental states has kept her alive. If you don't believe this, then you'd have to say that Sam has died and been replaced by a very good copy. If *you* were Sam, wouldn't you want to know the answer before you agreed to the procedure?

TIME

People often talk about time as if it were a thing. It flows, it passes, and we move through it. It also *seems* to go in one direction – from past to present to future. But do these common-sense ideas about time make philosophical sense?

We think of events using the terms **past**, **present** and **future**. We also say that time flows in one specific direction: event A must happen first, *then* event B, *then* C.

NOW

Event A	Event B	Event C
I drank some tea.	I am reading this book.	I will text my friend.
Past	Present	Future

Events also *change* their positions. When I was drinking tea, reading this book was future. Later on it became present, then past. Similarly, texting my friend will eventually be present, and then later on, past.

NOW

Event A	Event B	Event C
I drank some tea.	I read this book.	I am texting my friend.
Past	Past	Present

So far so good... or is it? British philosopher J.M.E. McTaggart argued that this idea of time involves a **contradiction**. If something involves a contradiction, it means it's saying two things are true that can't *both* be true. This suggests that time itself doesn't make sense! In fact, time must be *unreal*.

> **Now hang on a moment! What contradiction?**

> Well we've just said that *all events* have *all the properties* of past, present and future.

> But these properties are incompatible. One event can't be past *and* present *and* future.

> **Well, no, not *at the same time*, but...**

> ...but it's *time* we are trying to explain! You can't use it to explain itself. That's circular!

> **Can't we say that an event *was* future, *is* present and *will be* past?**

> Still circular! But even if it weren't, events change. The event that's present now will become present-in-the-past...

> ...but nothing can be both present-in-the-present *and* present-in-the-past.

> **You're losing me...**

> And it's no use saying 'no, not at the same time'. You'll just get another contradiction and another...

> **Oh dear.**

Philosophers have suggested various ways out of this. For example, some say that only the present exists. It doesn't make sense to say that things are past or future. Others suggest that *nothing* is past, present or future *full stop*. It's just all relative to where *you* are in time. Confused? You are not alone. As medieval philosopher, St. Augustine said,

> What then is time? If no one asks me, I know what it is. If I wish to explain it to him who asks, I do not know.

> In other words, time seems really obvious and simple as long as you don't have to explain it!

TIME TRAVEL

Time travel makes for exciting stories. But the idea of time travel brings up serious philosophical problems, which suggest that it's not logically possible. And if it's not logically possible, it's not *physically* possible either (whatever physicists say).

So what counts as time travel? Well, technically we are all travelling through time. Since you started reading this book, you have travelled into the future. But what people usually mean by time travel is travelling in the wrong direction – into the past – or into the future at a faster rate than everyone else. It's this sort of 'time travel' that creates **paradoxes** – scenarios that seem both possible and impossible.

ROUND AND ROUND AND ROUND AND...

Arthur travels to the future in a time machine and steals the blueprint for a time machine. He then goes back and gives it to Professor Wells, who uses it to build the time machine that took Arthur to the future. This scenario involves something called a **causal loop**. That's when events ultimately seem to cause themselves.

I found some blueprints for a time machine!

Finished! Let's test it out

In the distant future...

Phew! I found the blue prints. Professor Wells will need these to build the time machine.

THE GRANDFATHER PARADOX

Imagine Arthur travels back to a time before his grandfather had children, with the intention of killing him. But, if Arthur kills his grandfather, Arthur's *father* will not be born and nor will *Arthur*. So how *can* he kill his grandfather?

"But why *can't* Arthur kill his grandfather? What's stopping him – the laws of logic?!"

"Well maybe not, but there is still a problem. Before Arthur tries to do anything he can both kill his grandfather..."

"...and **cannot** (if Arthur kills him, then he won't *exist* to go back in time to kill him). This is a **logical contradiction**."

Some people say they have solved the Grandfather Paradox. Arthur *can* travel to the past and kill his grandfather, if the act of murder creates a *new* universe in which events happen differently. In this universe, Arthur will not be born, but he can exist in *this* universe, if he travels there from the universe in which he was born.

"Hmm. It seems odd to introduce this as an explanation for something which, as far as we know, hasn't happened."

"True. The best we can really say is that, *if* parallel universes exist, then maybe time travel, in this sense, is possible."

"Although it's not really **time travel**, anyway, is it? It's more multi-universe travel."

But even if time travel *is* logically possible, we still have another question to ask:

WHERE ARE ALL THE TIME TRAVELLERS?

In June 2009, physicist Stephen Hawking sent out invitations welcoming 'all future time travellers' to a party. But, the party had already happened and, not surprisingly, no one had turned up. Hawking's point was that if time travel *is* possible, at some point, someone will do it – so we'd expect to meet people from the future in the present. Simple, isn't it?

103

- IS THE MEANING OF 'DOG' THE OBJECT IT REFERS TO?
- ARE SENTENCES ALWAYS EITHER TRUE OR FALSE?
- IS IT LOGICAL TO BELIEVE THAT SOMETHING WILL HAPPEN AGAIN IF IT'S HAPPENED MANY TIMES BEFORE?

LOGIC AND LANGUAGE

At the heart of philosophy are the words and language we use to express an idea or argument. But our choice of words and the way we use them can differ from one person to the next.
So how do we know what *anyone* really means? And how can we rely on philosophy, if its central tools – words – can be so easily misunderstood?

To find the answers, many philosophers look closely at language itself. They break it down into parts and use the tools of logic – premises, conclusions and so on – to see if one thing truly does follow from another.

DIFFERENT WAYS OF REASONING

Philosophy, like mathematics, follows certain rules. It often involves reasoning from a set of **premises** to a **conclusion** that follows logically from them. Consider this simple conversation:

Did someone knock at the door?

Fuzzy always barks when someone is at the door.

Fuzzy didn't bark.

Therefore no one is at the door.

A philosopher might break down this conversation using logic (see pages 10-11), or, to use another phrase, **deductive reasoning**. It works like this...

PREMISE 1	PREMISE 2	CONCLUSION
Fuzzy always barks when someone is at the door.	Fuzzy didn't bark.	No one is at the door.

The advantage of deductive reasoning is its certainty. If the premises are true, and the overall argument is valid, then it follows logically that the conclusion must be true.

Of course, if one or even both premises are *false*, then the argument fails. For example, maybe Fuzzy doesn't *always* bark when someone is at the door...

REASONING BASED ON EXPERIENCE

Inductive reasoning is another form of argument. It uses evidence from the world around us, and observations from our senses, to lead to *probable* conclusions.

"Every time we've been to the cafe before midday, it's been nice and quiet."

"Great, it's 10 am now, so we *should* find a free table."

The statement that 'the cafe has been quiet before midday' is based on observing this many times. From this, you can conclude the same will *probably* happen again.

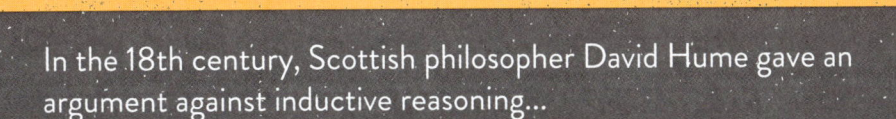

In the 18th century, Scottish philosopher David Hume gave an argument against inductive reasoning...

"The Sun will rise over that hill tomorrow."

"How do you know it really will rise tomorrow?"

"It's risen every day of my life so far. So of course it will rise tomorrow! That's inductive reasoning."

"Your belief is only justified if the future will resemble the past. But you can't assume that. You only believe it because it always has..."

Just because something has happened in the past *doesn't* always mean it will happen again. But the fact is that we *do* believe the Sun will rise tomorrow. Although inductive reasoning doesn't give us certainty, it seems we can't help using it in our day-to-day thinking.

THE PROBLEM WITH TRUTH

Does language follow logical rules? If it does, some philosophers argue, then it should be possible to break it down into sentences that are true or false. Looking for truth, however, can lead to contradictions. Consider this riddle, known as **the liar's paradox**...

THIS SENTENCE IS FALSE.

Is this true or false?

Well if it's true, then what it's saying must be false. But if the statement is false then the sentence is actually telling the truth. Hang on a minute...

↑
THAT SENTENCE ISN'T TRUE.

So if it's true, it's false, and if it's false, it's true?

Er... yes!

But nothing can be true AND false at the same time! That doesn't make sense.

In this example, it's tricky – perhaps impossible – to say whether the sentence itself is either true or false. Perhaps logic doesn't work for all sentences?

THE MEANING OF A WORD

What is the meaning of a word? Perhaps it's the physical object that the word refers to. On this view, the meaning of 'Everest' is a mountain. But you might suggest that the meaning of 'Everest' is also an idea, or a piece of information about it, such as 'the world's highest mountain'.

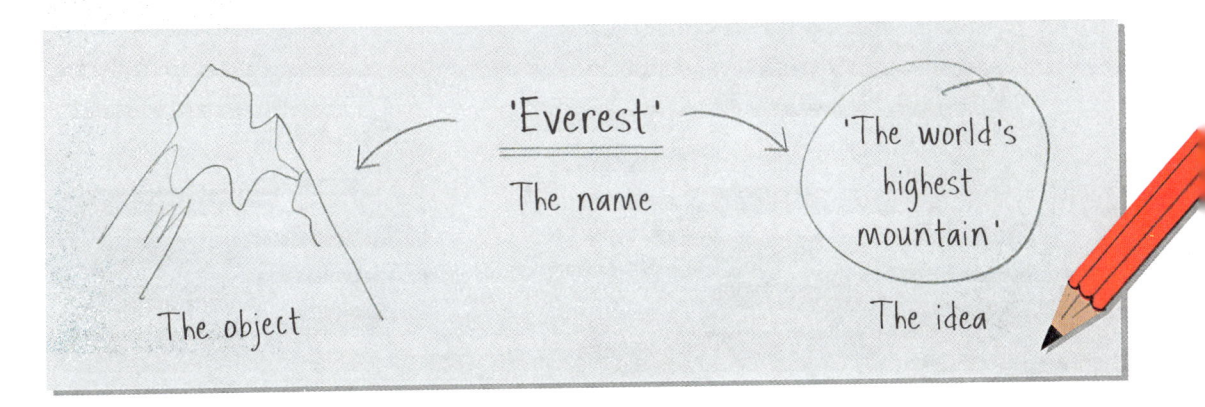

'Everest'
The name

The object

'The world's highest mountain'
The idea

Both types of meaning are acceptable, but they are very different. 'Everest' refers to a mountain in the Himalayas, whereas the phrase 'the world's highest mountain' *could* have referred to a mountain elsewhere.

Consider a cat called Basil. Basil likes to chase cars. He also likes to sleep on people's doorsteps.

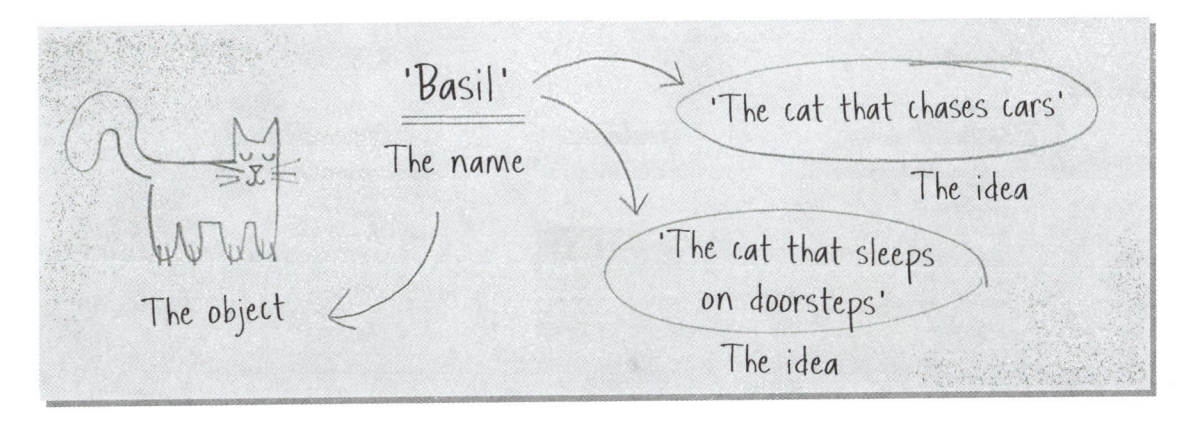

'Basil'
The name

The object

'The cat that chases cars'
The idea

'The cat that sleeps on doorsteps'
The idea

'The cat that chases cars' has a different meaning from 'The cat that sleeps on doorsteps'. Yet both sentences refer to the same thing, Basil. This shows how meaning can be looked at in multiple ways. But does it make sense to seek the precise meaning of a word? Turn the page to see another way of looking at it.

MEANING IS USE

Some philosophers have rejected the idea that words and language have a fixed meaning. They argue that the meaning of a word depends on its *use* in a sentence, the way it's expressed, the language itself...

How was your journey?

Very quick! I took a bus then walked five minutes.

No, I mean how was your *journey*?

Oh, my journey in life! It's been very hard, I took a long time to get here.

Here you can see how slippery meaning can be. So does it make sense to look for the meaning of a word independently of its context? Maybe not.

We're going to have a party this weekend.

The meaning of a word can also depend on the audience. One person's idea of a party might look very different to someone else's. So how do we ever really know we are talking about the same thing? The answer is, perhaps we don't.

MEANING AND THE AUTHOR

Any words you *read* have been written by someone: an author. When trying to understand a piece of writing, can you do so without considering what the author really means? Some people believe you *can*. They believe that meaning is based purely on the writing, NOT the writer.

ALICE'S ADVENTURES IN WONDERLAND — Lewis Carroll

- I think it's about a girl who falls down a rabbit hole.
- It's about the confusing advice that adults give you.
- It's about growing up and the quest for true knowledge.
- For me, it's about the dangers of taking drugs.

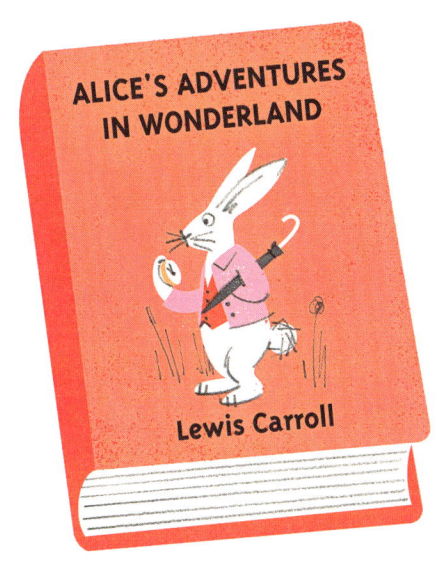

Many books contain hidden and multiple meanings that can be endlessly interpreted. So perhaps it doesn't matter what the author intended, as long as the reader can back up their own opinion of what the book is *really* about.

But sometimes knowing something about an author can change your point of view – so maybe it does matter.

CROW — Ted Hughes

- This author writes a lot about crows. He must really like birds.
- But he wrote that after his wife died. I think the crow is a symbol of death.

DOES LIFE HAVE A BIGGER PURPOSE?
WHERE DOES THE UNIVERSE COME FROM?
CAN PHILOSOPHY HELP ME *FEEL* BETTER?

THE MEANING OF LIFE

Philosophy often looks at aspects of life, such as art, ethics or knowledge. But what about how it all fits together? So far we have looked at philosophy as something to do – a hobby or perhaps a job. But for some people, philosophy isn't just an activity or a way of thinking – it can provide a code to live by. For many people, philosophy is a way of living.

THE GOOD LIFE?

In pursuit of wisdom and a life of virtue, some ancient philosophers gave up their wealth, or left their homes, to live very disciplined lives. For them, philosophy was a practical way to transform themselves into, they hoped, better people.

Epicurean: The good life means being free from pain in the body and mind. We live simply and enjoy the company of our friends.

Stoic: Don't concern yourself with external circumstances. Accept reality whether it is pleasant or not. Act virtuously.

Ancient Sceptic: We are investigators. We try not to believe anything we do not know for certain.

This isn't just something people did thousands of years ago. Philosophers from the last century also sought to change their lives with philosophy – but with a little less discipline.

Existentialist: Take responsibilty for all your choices. Don't forget that you are free to make your own life!

Phenomenologist: I pay careful attention to anything and everything – from coffee to rain. Then I describe how I experience it.

Perhaps the most famous example of a philosopher who *lived* his philosophy is Socrates. He didn't earn a living. He didn't participate in city politics. He didn't even wear shoes. Instead, he spent his life wandering around the city, challenging people's beliefs and pursuing knowledge.

I neither know about virtue nor think I know.

Well, I *do* know about virtue.

You *do*? I have a *lot* of questions for you then.

If you're interested in pursuing philosophy as a way of life, you don't have to walk around barefoot or give up your belongings. You just have to examine your beliefs. Make your life a process of exploration.

Is it better to have a set of beliefs or to examine your beliefs constantly, and change them?

Is it possible to believe nothing at all?

Should I define myself according to what I do? Should I define myself *at all*?

Do people have to behave in a certain way?

Is there a better way to organize a society?

It's OK to admit that you're unsure or that you don't know something. In fact, the moment you do, you've taken the first step towards knowledge and discovery. And you've found something to do – discover answers to new questions.

WHAT IS THE MEANING OF LIFE?

When people think of philosophy, this is often *the* question that comes to mind.

When I look up at the sky and the stars, I think of how vast the universe is and how small we are. I wonder what it all means?

I'm not sure what you *mean by that.*

I want an explanation for the universe, so that it makes sense to me.

Is that too much to ask?

Some people look for meaning by trying to understand why we exist at all. And that means explaining what the universe itself is.

Some explain it in terms of its history – or where it came from.

The universe began with a big bang and has been expanding ever since.

Others talk about its purpose – or where it is going.

I think the universe will eventually collapse on itself in a big crunch. Maybe this *is the purpose of the universe...*

But, if anything, these explanations leave us with more questions. *Why* was there a big bang? *What happens after the universe collapses*? Is there any purpose to this whole mess?

Most explanations need *further* explanation. Whatever story you are told about life's meaning, you can always ask why *that* story is the case and be told *another* story.

Or, as philosophers might put it, it's a problem of infinite regress.

> Why was there a big bang?
>
> Well before that everything was incredibly hot and dense and then it exploded.
>
> But why?
>
> We don't know. Perhaps we can explain *how*, but not *why*. If you keep asking, I'll just give another explanation and you'll ask me to explain *that* one.
>
> But then, is there any way to answer my original question?

WHAT'S THE MEANING OF... A POTATO?

Seems like a pointless question, right? I can tell you stories about a potato, but ultimately, it's just a potato. The universe is like a potato, in the sense that, asking what it's all about, is like asking what a potato means. It's just *there*. At some point you have to stop asking *why*.

> Behold the potato! I'm not sure why it's here, but it's great anyway.

> BEHOLD!

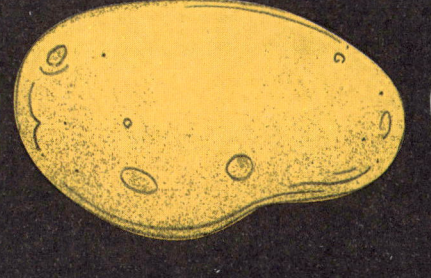

Maybe this isn't a satisfying answer to the question. But there's a reason for this. Usually when people ask, what is the meaning of life, they're actually asking something else. Turn over to explore the *real* question.

WHAT MAKES MY *LIFE* MEANINGFUL?

Some experiences in our lives are *so* interesting and engaging that it's as if nothing else matters. At times when we *don't* feel engaged, we might wonder why we're here. So what makes life *feel* meaningful?

YOU MAKE IT MEANINGFUL

One idea is that YOU decide what makes your experience feel rich and vivid. You decide why you're here. You decide the meaning of *your* life.

It's all about what you choose to do. I decide what makes my life meaningful. So I choose to...

...sing to lions.

Grrrrr!

AAAAAAAAAA!

Wait, even if I make a choice, it seems that some actions are more sensible than others.

If I don't want to suffer, then I need to act sensibly...

...but then, it looks as if I don't really get to choose.

It seems we don't have the freedom to choose just *anything* for our lives. Perhaps some choices are more sensible, or meaningful, than others.

DOING THE RIGHT THINGS

Some philosophers think there are certain things that make life meaningful, and some things that *don't*. But, they rarely agree on what those things are.

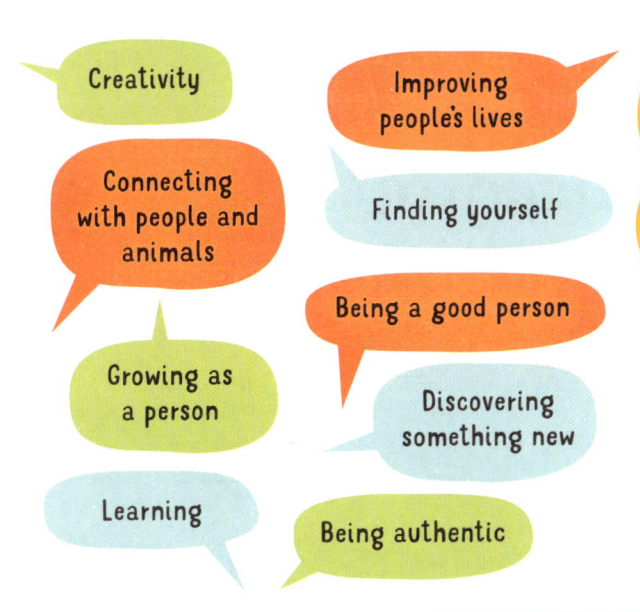

- Creativity
- Improving people's lives
- Connecting with people and animals
- Finding yourself
- Being a good person
- Growing as a person
- Discovering something new
- Learning
- Being authentic

> I think it's possible to do these things and still not have a sense of wonder or engagement...
>
> ...and I'm not sure what some of this advice *actually* means.

THERE IS NO MEANING – AND THAT'S OK

These approaches both assume that life must be *made* meaningful – that unless you do *something*, your life is meaningless. But is this true? Maybe life is already rich enough. Maybe our expectations of what life *could* be gets in the way of what life already *is*.

Typically, people consider some things to be meaningful, but not others.

> But are we right to do this? Even simple events can be magical experiences.

Experiment and see for yourself. Pay attention to something simple, such as the feel of the pages of this book, or the path of a raindrop. When you pay close attention, what is your experience like? Is it engaging?

WHAT NEXT?

Philosophy can be difficult. If it were easy, we'd already know the answers to life's big questions. So, if you've found yourself scratching your head a few times while reading this book, congratulations! It means you've been reading it correctly.

But now that you know a little about what philosophy is, and how it works, what can you actually *do* with it? Apart from annoying your family and teachers, that is...

> Put those books down and finish your homework!

> There are two of us and only one of you, and *neither* of us wants to do our homework. So it's a greater good for a greater number if we *don't*.

> The future will become the past, so at some point my homework will have been done even if I don't do it now.

> I read that we can never really *know* anything – so what's the point of going to school to learn?

> Who gets to choose which facts are worth knowing anyway?

> It's not my fault I'm late, Miss. The universe was set up in such a way that I was always going to be late this morning.

If you really want to get into philosophy, a simple way to start is to read more books. Turn to page 125 for a list of some of the most influential thinkers in history, then see what you can find out about their ideas.

But the best way to *do* philosophy is to argue with people. Remember, an **argument** is the word philosophers use to describe a set of premises and a conclusion. It doesn't mean they like shouting at each other – although plenty of real philosophers do that, too. If you have an argument, test it out on someone. If they say it has an error, try to defend your argument, or improve it – but be polite. Where? Well, your school or local library might have a philosophy society you can join, or you might be able to start one up yourself.

WHY BOTHER?

After reading this book, we hope you've been persuaded that philosophy is interesting, fun and sometimes even useful.
Here are a few quotations from philosophers about their subject.

Science is what you know. Philosophy is what you don't know.

Philosophy begins in wonder.

The only thing I know is that I know nothing.

Philosophy means living among ice and high mountains – seeking out everything strange and questionable in existence.

The real sign of intelligence isn't knowledge, it's *imagination*.

Life will be lived all the better if it has no meaning.

MULTIPLE MYSTERIES

If there's one thing philosophers love, it's coming up with mysteries, puzzles and paradoxes. Here are just a few to test your philosophical skills. Some are thought to be unsolvable – but people have suggested possible answers to almost all of these questions.

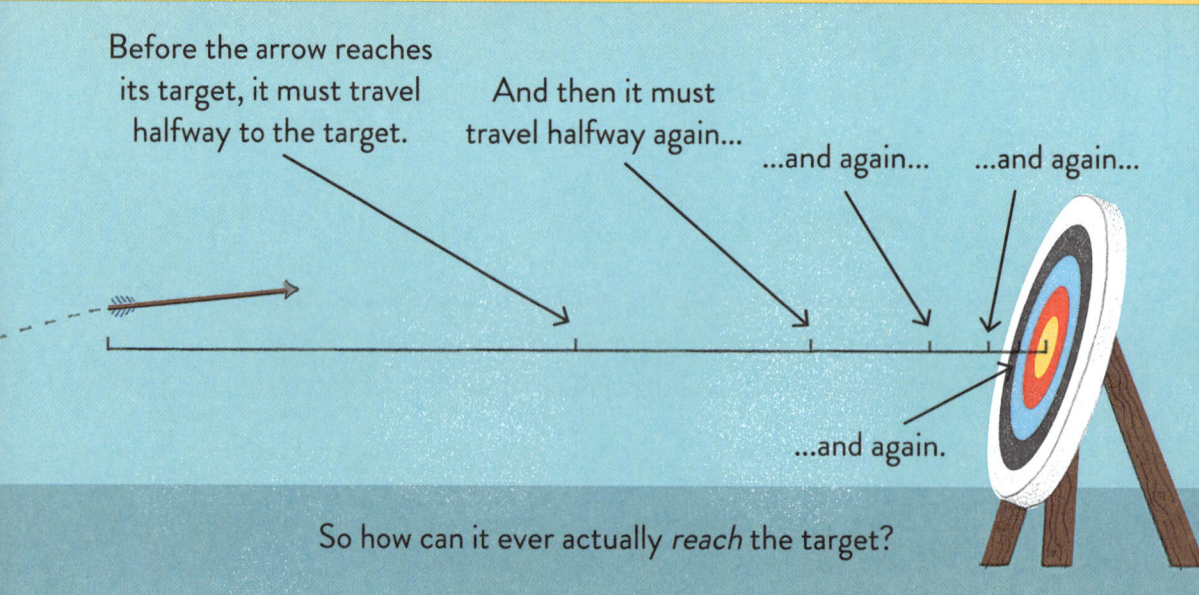

Before the arrow reaches its target, it must travel halfway to the target.

And then it must travel halfway again...

...and again...

...and again...

...and again.

So how can it ever actually *reach* the target?

When you think, are your thoughts made using language, or are some thoughts possible with no language?

I *think* so, but I can't describe those thoughts without using language. Not fair!

When does orange...

...become yellow?

"How could you tell if your family was replaced by incredibly lifelike robots?"

"And would it matter if they were?"

"If the universe and everything in it was doubling in size every second, would it be possible to tell?"

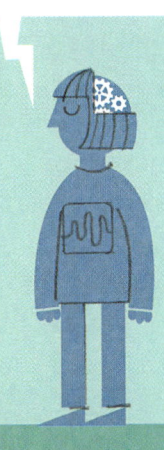

"Argh! My measuring tape keeps getting bigger!"

"Imagine there's a town with one barber in it. He *only* shaves people who *don't* shave themselves."

"Is that barber allowed to shave himself?"

"Wait, if the barber doesn't shave himself, then he needs to go to a barber to be shaved. And he's the only barber in town."

"But if he *does* shave himself, then he's breaking his own rule. I'm so confused!"

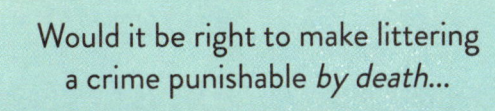

Would it be right to make littering a crime punishable *by death*...

...if you knew *for certain* that this would stop people from ever littering?

GLOSSARY

This glossary explains some of the words used in this book. Words written in *italic* type are explained in other entries.

aesthetics the study of beauty and art.
argument an attempt to reach a particular *conclusion*, usually based on a set of *premises*.
circular argument an *argument* whose *premises* start off by assuming that the conclusion is true.
coherent when a set of ideas or beliefs all support each other.
conclusion the result of an *argument* after following through its *premises*.
consistent when a set of claims do not contradict each other.
deductive reasoning arriving at a *conclusion* based purely on *logic*.
determinism a belief that everything that happens is predictable, based on the laws of nature, and on the state of the Universe when it began.
ethics the study of right and wrong, good and bad, duties and responsibilities.
free will the ability to choose to do one thing rather than another.
identity what makes a thing itself, or a person who they are.
inductive reasoning arriving at a *conclusion* based on past experiences.
infinite regress an *argument* that has no firm *foundation*, but always relies on some further piece of *justification*.
invalid an *argument* whose *conclusion* does not *logically* follow from the stated *premises*.
justification an explanation for why something is the case.
legitimate in politics, something that people agree has a right to be the way that it is.
logic a formal system for testing that *arguments* are valid.
meaning how words are used by some and understood by others.
morals ways of acting and behaving that most people in a society agree are good or proper.
objective truly independent of any one person's point of view.
paradox a statement that appears to be true, but that also contradicts itself.
paternalism setting rules that limit people's freedom, supposedly for their own good.
premise a statement that claims to be true.
scepticism taking the view that nobody knows anything for certain.
sound an *argument* whose *premises* are true and whose *conclusion* follows *logically*.
subjective true only relative to one person's point of view.
unsound an *argument* whose *premises* are not all true, or whose *conclusion* is not *logically* implied by the premises.
valid an *argument* whose *conclusion* follows *logically* follow its *premises*.

FAMOUS PHILOSOPHERS

Throughout this book, we've described ideas developed by lots of philosophers. Chapter by chapter, here are their names, and the times and places where they lived. Some appear more than once.

WHAT IS PHILOSOPHY?
David Hume (Scotland 1711-1776); Socrates (Athens, roughly 470-400BC)

KNOWLEDGE
Al-Ghazali (Seljuk Empire 1053-1111); George Berkeley (Ireland and England 1685-1753); René Descartes (France and the Netherlands 1596-1650); Gottlob Frege (Germany 1848-1925); Edmund Gettier (USA 1927-present day); Bertrand Russell (UK 1872-1970)

MIND
Elisabeth of Bohemia (Saxony 1618-1680); René Descartes; Hilary Putnam (USA 1926-2016);

BEAUTY AND ART
Alan Goldman (USA 1945-present day); Immanuel Kant (Germany, 1724-1804); Plato (Athens roughly 425-370BC); John Ruskin (UK 1819-1900)

GOD
Anselm of Canterbury (England, roughly 1030-1100); Augustine of Hippo (North Africa 354-430); Blaise Pascal (France 1623-1662)

POLITICS
Thomas Hobbes (England 1588-1679); Hannah Arendt (Germany and USA 1906-1975); John Locke (England 1632-1704); Karl Marx (Germany and UK 1818-1883); John Stuart Mill (UK 1806-1873); Mary Warnock (UK, 1924-2019)

HOW TO BE GOOD
Aristotle (Athens roughly 385-320BC); Jeremy Bentham (UK 1748-1832); Confucius (China roughly 550-475BC); Philippa Foot (UK 1920-2010); Immanuel Kant; Søren Kierkegaard (Denmark 1813-1855); John Stuart Mill; Judith Jarvis Thomson (USA 1929-present day)

TIME AND IDENTITY
Elisabeth of Bohemia; John Locke; J. M. E. McTaggart (UK 1866-1925); Bernard Williams (UK 1929-2003)

LOGIC AND LANGUAGE
Roland Barthes (France 1915-1980); Noam Chomsky (USA 1928-present day) Jacques Derrida (Algeria and France, 1930-2004); Gottlob Frege; David Hume; Bertrand Russell; Ludwig Wittgenstein (Austria and UK 1889-1951)

THE MEANING OF LIFE
Siddhartha Guatama, the Buddha (India, roughly 480-400BC); Jean-Paul Sartre (France 1905-1980); Simone de Beauvoir (France 1908-1986)

INDEX

absolutism, moral, 87
actions, 31, 32, 34, 36, 38, 39, 78, 82, 84, 86, 118
aesthetics, 41-51
aliens, 5, 33, 35
animals, 5, 33, 35
Anselm of Canterbury, 62
arguments, 8, 9, 10-11, 15, 106, 121
art, 41, 48-51
   performance, 51
Augustine, St., 101

basic beliefs, 22
beauty, 41-51
brain in a jar, 12, 18-19, 23
brains, 14, 33, 34, 35, 96, 97, 99

capital punishment, 90, 123
causal loops, 102
causal theory of knowledge, 26-27
certainty, 8, 18, 106, 107
chance, 38, 60, 61
change, 94-95
circular arguments, 21, 99, 101
coherence, 23
common sense, 19, 31, 100
computers, 18, 19, 23, 35, 97, 99
conclusions, 10, 106
consciousness, continuity of, 98-99
consequences, 82-83
consistency, 23
contradictions, 56, 100, 101, 103, 108
cosmological argument, 63

deductive reasoning, 106
deontology, 84
design, argument from, 60-61
desires, 32, 33, 34, 35

determinism, 36, 38-39
Duchamp, Marcel, 50
equality, 68-71
ethics, 77-91
euthanasia, 90
evil, 58-59
evolution, 60
experiences, 98, 99

foundationalism, 21, 22
free will, 7, 36-39, 59
freedom, 7, 39, 72-73, 118
functionalism, 34-35

God, 5, 6, 52-63, 80
   arguments for the existence of, 60-63
Golden Mean, 44
Goldman, Alvin, 27
good, 54, 58, 59, 77-91
goodness, 54, 58
governments, 5, 7, 65, 67, 73-75

happiness, 70, 82, 83, 88
Hawking, Stephen, 103
Hume, David, 107

identity, 93, 94-99
   numerical, 94, 95
   personal, 96-99
      bodily, 96
      physical, 96-97
      psychological, 97, 98-99
   qualitative, 94, 95
impossibility, 56
inductive reasoning, 107
infinite regress, 20
justice, 36, 37
justified true belief, 25

Kant, Immanuel, 46
knowledge, 17-27
  theories of, 24-27

language, 37, 105, 109, 110-111
laws, 72, 73, 74, 75, 91
legitimacy, 74, 75
logic, 10-11, 56, 105

Mctaggart, J.M.E., 100-101
meaning
  artistic, 49, 50
  of life, 113-119
  words, 109, 110-111
medical ethics, 91
memories, 98, 99
mental states, 33, 34, 35, 97, 99
metaphysics, 93
mind, philosophy of 28-39
mind-body problem, 32-33
  identity theory, 33
minds, 30-33, 96, 98
  other, 30-31
moral codes, 77, 78, 80
moral questions, 90-91
moral rules, 78, 79
moral theory *see* ethics

objectivity, 43, 44, 46, 47
omnipotence, 54, 55-57, 58
omniscience, 54, 58
ontological argument, 62

pain, 33, 35
paradoxes, 55, 56, 57, 102, 103, 108, 122
  Grandfather, 102-103
  of omnipotence, 55-57
  of time travel, 102-103
  the Liar's, 108
parallel universes, 103

Pascal, Blaise, 63
Pascal's Wager, 63
paternalism, 72-73
perfect being, 54
Plato, 47
pleasure, 47
police, 74, 75
political theory, 65-75
premises, 10, 11, 55, 105, 106
privacy, 91
probability, 38, 60, 61, 107
problem of evil, 57, 58-59
property, private, 66-67

relativism, moral, 86
religious experience, 63
rights, 5, 77, 83, 87, 90
robots, 14, 35, 123
rules, 73, 74-75

sceptical arguments, 18-19, 21
selflessness, 81
social contract, 75
society, 14, 65, 66, 67, 68, 72, 75
Socrates, 9, 115
Socratic Method, 9
soundness, 11, 106
subjectivity, 43, 45

thought experiments, 12-13, 33, 61, 66, 96, 97, 99
time, 93, 100-101
time travel, 102-103
truth, 108

utilitarianism, 81, 82-83
validity, 11, 106
values, 77
virtue ethics, 85
war, 91

ACKNOWLEDGEMENTS

Written by
Jordan Akpojaro, Rachel Firth
and Minna Lacey

Illustrated by
Nick Radford

Edited by
Alex Frith

Designed by
Freya Harrison

Philosophy consultant:
Dr Alex Kaiserman,
University of Oxford

Series editor: Jane Chisholm

Series designer:
Stephen Moncrieff

The websites recommended at Usborne Quicklinks are regularly reviewed but Usborne Publishing is not responsible and does not accept liability for the availability or content of any website other than its own, or for any exposure to harmful, offensive or inaccurate material which may appear on the Web. Usborne Publishing will have no liability for any damage or loss caused by viruses that may be downloaded as a result of browsing the sites it recommends.

First published in 2020 by Usborne Publishing Ltd., Usborne House, 83-85 Saffron Hill, London, EC1N 8RT, United Kingdom.
usborne.com
Copyright © 2020 Usborne Publishing Ltd. The name Usborne and the devices ⊕ ⊗ are Trade Marks of Usborne Publishing Ltd. All rights reserved. No part of this publication may be reproduced, stored in any retrieval system, or transmitted in any form or by any means, electronic, mechanical, photocopying, recording or otherwise, without the prior permission of the publisher. UKE.